CONSTANTINOPLE:

The Way It Was
and
The Green Mosque at Bursa

Translated and annotated by David Ball

Pierre Loti

CONSTANTINOPLE:

The Way It Was
and
The Green Mosque at Bursa

Translated and annotated by David Ball

ISBN 9944-393-02-9

Published by Amphora Eğitim Yayıncılık Tur. ve Tic. Ltd. Şti.
Gümüşsuyu Karyağdı Sok. No: 1
Eyüp - İstanbul
Tel.: (212) 545 17 58
Fax: (212) 563 49 65
e-mail: editionsamphora@superonline.com
İstanbul, October 2006

The first English translation of *Constantinople en 1890* was published by Ünlem Basim Yayincilik in 2002; it has been revised by the translator for this edition.

Printed in Turkey by MAS Matbaacılık A.Ş.
Dereboyu Cad. Zagra İş Mrk.
B Blok No: 1
Maslak - 34398 İstanbul
Tel.: (212) 285 11 96
Fax: (212) 276 59 55
e-mail:info@masmat.com.tr

CONTENTS

PIERRE LOTI AND ISTANBUL

Pierre Loti (1850-1923) is not as well known today as he used to be, even to the French reader. He was one of those rare authors whose books, as well as his personality and his hectic life, fascinated the public during his lifetime. He was a famous man; articles and news about him (true or false) appeared in magazines and newspapers continually, and so did his photograph. Like movie actors or rock stars today, he was an artist whose life and behavior fascinated the general public. It is said that when he was the captain of the *Vautour* (the stationary escort vessel of the French embassy in Constantinople), Istanbul ladies had him followed so as not to miss the slightest detail of his conduct and his dress.

Born Jules Viaud, Pierre Loti pursued a naval career before making a name for himself among the best known reporters and artists of the contemporary Paris press and then gaining fame in the world of letters. His initial contact with Turkey came in 1870, when the training ship *Jean Bart*, on which he was sailing as a cadet midshipman, made a stopover in Izmir. Aside from this brief stop, he had seven stays in Turkey, the first in 1876 and the last in 1913. All in all, they add up to almost three years.

After a number of trips to Tahiti, where the ladies-in-waiting of Queen Pomare baptized him Loti, after the name of a tropical flower he would use to sign his works later on-he went to Senegal, where he was irremediably shattered by a failed love affair. In the spring of 1876 his naval career brought him first to Salonica and then to Istanbul, the capital of the Ottoman Empire at the time. He would remain attached to Istanbul all his life.

A city where eastern and western cultures come together, a city torn between modernity and tradition, Istanbul is a presence in Loti's life and work from his first to his last book (*Aziyadé* and *Suprêmes Visions d'Orient* respectively), as well as in *Fantôme d'Orient*, *Les Désenchantées* (published in English as *The Unawakened*, 1906), *Turquie agonisante* (*Turkey Is Dying*) and many other texts.

The bitter memories of his Senegalese love still weighed on him in Salonica; after that failure "he was looking for adventure, for the unusual-out of bravado, and the defiant attitude of a rejected lover."[1] When he met Aziyadé, "a Turkish woman who was a Turk's wife,"[2] it gave his life a new meaning, and confirmed his attachment to Turkey. What had been for him at first only "an intoxication of the imagination and the senses"[3] changed into a passion that permeated his whole life.

After Julien Viaud had left Salonica to serve on the *Gladiateur*, which guarded the French embassy in Istanbul, Aziyadé's husband Abeddin moved his harem to the Ottoman capital and the two lovers were able to continue their illicit meetings.

Built on the two banks of the Bosphorus along the Golden Horn and the Sea of Marmara, the city that was then called both Constantinople and Stamboul was huge, if we include its poorer outlying districts. The Bosphorus is the name of the strait that links the Black Sea to the Sea of Marmara, which in turn separates two continents: Asia and Europe; the Golden Horn is merely a sound, located at the mouth of the Bosphorus on its European side. The neighborhood on the right bank of the Golden Horn covers the ancient triangular city of Constantinople. This was the old Muslim city called Stamboul, bristling with minarets and domes. The neighborhood of Pera, on the left bank of the Golden Horn, was the Levantine neighborhood, where the Christian population lived. The name Constantinople used to refer to the whole city, while the name Stamboul tended to mean the neighborhood on the right bank. Today the Turks use only the name Istanbul for the whole city.

The first images that remained in the memory of the "poor young officer" reveal no enthusiasm for the city, where he "[didn't] know a soul." (*Aziyadé.*) Little by little, he grew accustomed to oriental life, began to wear a caftan and a fez, went to the Karagez shadow theater, smoked a hookah and went to live in Eyub, "the heart of Islam in Europe, buried in a kind of gloomy hedged farmland that borders the great cemeteries surrounded by graves." As [he saw] more of Turkish life, he "[grew] fonder and fonder of this dreamy, proud people."[4] Although sometimes he could no longer take himself seriously in his "Turkish role," he never stopped playing this exotic role, so that little by little he became a Turk.[5]

His idyll with Aziyadé was the source of his first book, *Aziyadé.* In his own judgment, it is "a senseless novel! a love poem sung in the midst of the springtime, in the midst of danger, in the midst of the East and the midst

---

1 Pierre-Edouard Briquet, *Pierre Loti et l'Orient*, Zeluck, Paris,1946,p. 293.
2 Loti, *Aziyadé.*
3 *Ibid.*
4 Loti, *Constantinople in 1890.*
5 Alain Quella-Villéger, *Pierre Loti, le pèlerin de la planète,* Auberon, Paris, 1988, p. 77.

of the Islamic reawakening!"[6] When he returned from Istanbul shortly before the Turco-Russian War in 1877, Julien Viaud felt the need to "sing his pain, to shout it aloud to unknown passersby"[7] in order to get rid of the heavy weight of the past that had descended upon him. The diary he'd kept regularly ever since his early youth enabled him to turn it into a novel.

In general, the events related in the novel coincide with the truth, although he did have to modify them somewhat. In this novel practically devoid of plot, he showed his enthusiasm for the city in which he had "truly mingled with the life of the people"[8] through a series of tableaus that flash across the page like snapshots. True to his profession as artist-reporter, Julien Viaud transposes visual scenes and the great political events of the time into writing. He gives us a veritable theatrical production of the city itself. The novel appeared anonymously and passed almost unnoticed. His resounding success in the world of letters came the following year, with his *Le Mariage de Loti*, serialized in Madame Adam's *Nouvelle Revue.*

Aziyadé and Istanbul would stay with Pierre Loti for the rest of his life: the two names were inseparable for him. Ten years later, in 1887, he returned to the Ottoman capital. He had become famous and had admirers everywhere. Elizabeth of Romania (known in literature under her pen name, Carmen Sylva) invited him to the castle of Sinaïa; he took advantage of the occasion and went to Istanbul for the second time.

He was returning "to stir up all those ashes" of his youth (*Fantôme d'Orient.*) The memory of Aziyadé haunted him from the moment he left. He had a strange premonition that she was dead, and he wanted to persuade himself that she really was. He spent three days feverishly looking for clues and people who might be able to tell him what had happened to his beloved. After many adventures, his quest finally led him to the cemetery. From that time on, Aziyadé's grave would be his Mecca: he would go there every time he came back to Istanbul. The breathless narrative of his adventures would be material for another work: *Fantôme d'Orient.*

This "chronicle of a death foretold," as Nedim Gürsel calls it, marks the spot where a dream of love ends on a little grave in the Topkapi cemetery and launches Loti on another, greater dream that transcends and magnifies the one before it: love for Turkey.[9] Loti would become a writer committed to the Turkish cause, and the seeds of his Turkophilia were certainly planted by this love affair. Nonetheless, it would be a grave mistake to sum up his love for Turkey as the love he had for the young woman. "Islam cast a spell on me that will never leave me, at the time I was living

---

6 Loti, *Journal intime* (Diary), May 28, 1879.
7 Loti, *Fantôme d'Orient.*
8 *Ibid.*
9 Alain Quella-Villéger, *op. cit.*, p. 128.

on the banks of the Bosphorus," he confesses in *Fantôme d'Orient*; but it was a spell that grew with time, not love at first sight.

In 1889 the great publishing house Hachette asked him to contribute to the series of works it was devoting to "Capitals of the World." He agreed to write a presentation of the Ottoman capital, but first wanted to see Istanbul again: it had become the city that was dearest to him after Rochefort, his native town. Since the Queen of Romania had again invited him to stay with her, he went to Istanbul by way of Bucharest, as he had on his preceding visit, after a stop at the castle of Sinaïa. He stayed there for four days, May 12-15, at the Hôtel d'Angleterre. This third trip to Istanbul led to *Constantinople in 1890*,[10] published by Hachette in 1892 before it was collected in *L'Exilée* the following year.

The text begins with a suggestive evocation of the "the queen city of the East."[11] "Ah, Stamboul! Of all the names that can still enchant me, this one remains the most magical. As soon as I hear it, a vision appears before me: very, very high in the air, far off at first in the blurry distance, there is the suggestion of something gigantic, an incomparable outline of the city." (*Constantinople in 1890*, below, p. 15.) "Ah, Stamboul! Of all the names that can still enchant me, this one remains the most magical. As soon as I hear it, a vision appears before me: very, very high in the air, far off at first in the blurry distance, there is the suggestion of something gigantic, an incomparable outline of the city." (p. 15.) Then comes an orientalist painting where the traditional components of that outline reappear: the domes and minarets of the mosques, the multicolored crowds, the cypresses, the Bosphorus... More than "an impersonal description" of the ancient city, viewed with "artistic detachment," it is perceived "through [his] soul." (*Ibid.*) With little impressionist touches that stress the form of things, he translates his vision into emotional images, colored with memories. Then he begins a real chronicle, peppered with the events of his third stay in Istanbul. He takes his reader through the Grand Bazaar and the Topkapi Palace, plunges him into the tumult of Galata, tells him about his nocturnal jaunts away from his hotel...

In the course of the audience granted to him by the Sultan Abd-ul Hamid II in the Yildiz Palace, he "dare[s] to express all [his] melancholy regret in seeing the old things disappear" (p. 45), pours out his concerns about the rapid modernization of Istanbul. In this work, for the first time, he talks of tourists "spewed out" by the Orient-Express whom he sees "hurried [through the city] by shameless guides." (p. 38) He worries about the possible harmful

---

10 *Constantinople in 1890*, translated and annotated by David Ball, Ünlem Basım Yayıncılık, Istanbul, 2002, 55 pp. The present volume is a revised translation, with three additional essays.
11 *Constantinople in 1890*, see below, p. xxx.

effects of tourism. We should note that the Orient-Express went direct to Istanbul from Paris since 1899.

As he returned to France from a trip to the Holy Land in 1894, Loti stopped in Istanbul for two weeks. During this fourth stay, accompanied by Paul Cambon, the French Ambassador, he visited another Turkish city: Bursa. He describes his trip in *La Mosquée verte* (*The Green Mosque*,[12]) which appears at the end of his book *La Galilée*.

In 1903, Commander Julien Viaud returns to Istanbul. Now fifty-three, he takes command of the *Vautour*, stationary escort vessel of the French embassy. At the beginning of this fifth stay in the Ottoman capital, he leads a retired life and outside of his official duties, does not appear very much in public. He is careful not to get involved in any new adventure.

This calm life comes to an end when he receives a letter, apparently from a Turkish admirer. The woman who wrote it was not alone; there were three of them: a Frenchwoman-a journalist passing through Istanbul-and two Turkish sisters of French origin who had a European upbringing. In their meetings with Loti, the three young ladies pretend to be real Turks and talk to him about the social condition of Turkish women; they persuade him to write a novel that would express the suffering of a modern Muslim woman. Moreover, the French journalist who instigated this hoax would slip amorous insinuations into her letters and their meetings in order to recall Aziyadé, using the incognito of chadors and black veils. This adventure seems utterly uninteresting at first sight, yet in spite of this-and his own convictions-Pierre Loti made a best-seller out of it: the novel *Les Désenchantées* (translated as *The Unawakened*.) The hoax only became officially known after Loti's death, when Marc Hèlys published *Le Secret des "Désenchantées."*

In *Les Désenchantées*, Istanbul appears as a city whose tragic spell resides in its fragile beauty in the face of the aggressive, insistent West. In the regrets of this orientalist esthete, one can discern his awareness of a dying Turkey.[13] From now on, "More than ever, Stamboul produces the effect of a disappearing city, pathetically westernizing itself and plunging into banality, agitation and ugliness. Now one must make a constant, indulgent selection of what to look at, what parts to visit." (*Les Désenchantées*.)

In his retirement, Loti returned to Istanbul for the sixth time in his life, in 1910, and stayed there for nine weeks. The real reason for his trip was to penetrate the mystery surrounding the death or disappearance of Jenane, the heroine of *Les Désenchantées*. He was the guest of Countess Ostrorog in Kandili for a few days. Despite the kind intentions of a considerate hostess, he persisted in finding a place to stay in the heart of old Stamboul. Finally,

---

12 Translated in its entirety below, p. 71-93.
13 Alain Quella-Villéger, "Istanbul, le regard de Pierre Loti" in *Oluşum/Genèse*, 48-49, May-October 1997.

a young Turkish officer whose family was away agreed to rent him his house in Çemberlitas. The municipality of Istanbul put up a plaque there in July, 1920 to perpetuate the memory of the famous writer. Except for the Ostrorogs' *yali* (their majestic house by the sea), it is the only one of the Istanbul houses Loti lived in that can still be seen today.

Unlike what he had supposed, Loti returned to Istanbul for the last time in 1913, this time on an official visit at the invitation of men in governmental circles. He received a triumphant welcome. "The friend of our dark days," as he was then called in the Ottoman Empire, had stood up for the Turkish cause in his *Turquie agonisante* (*Turkey Is Dying*) during the 1911 Italo-Turkish war for Tripoli and the Balkan wars (1912, 1913.) He relates his two last trips in *Suprêmes Visions d'Orient*, the last book to appear during his lifetime. Despite his advanced age, he will untiringly defend "his second country" after the First World War (*La Mort de notre chère France en Orient*) when, with the Treaty of Sèvres, the attempt was made not only to cut Turkey off from Europe, but to eliminate it.

In his passionate pleas for the five hundred year old empire, the author of *Turkey Is Dying* denounces the imperialist ambitions of the great powers and laments the fact that "poor, great, majestic Stamboul" is wasting away. (*Turquie agonisante.*) Despite the less visible place that Istanbul occupies in these polemical works, when he does mention it his speech changes, taking on a virulent tone: "Will Europe understand that Stamboul, with a frightful threat hanging over it today, is a sacred place of history, art and poetry that must be defended at all costs? Will it understand that the day the crescent flies high above it no longer, its charm and magic will suddenly disappear? Of course not. Europe will not understand, and I am wasting my breath." (*Ibid.*)

In *Suprêmes Visions d'Orient*, Istanbul is no longer seen and described as a dream city, but as a rapidly declining city whose spell is dissipating as westernization progresses. "How uglier everything has become, how everything is vanishing! [. . .] the new Levantine buildings and the advertising posters of the German profiteers-they are quite simply hideous..." And yet, in this dying capital pervaded by the splendor of a glorious past, there are moments when he is lulled into thinking that the old East is not dead: "A warm, marvelous night, a magical night. Not a ripple troubles the pale mirror of the sea, and at the top of the sky, the great full moon of Ramadan gives a silvery sheen to all things. [. . .] the hills and woods of Europe and Asia draw sharp jagged shapes, almost black, on the very light sky, and the whiteness of the villages [of the Bosphorus] stand out in front of them-the domes of the mosques and high spires of the minarets." (*Suprêmes Visions.*)

Istanbul is not a city one can take in right away. According to Ahmet Hamdi, a contemporary Turkish author, this metropolis is like a capricious coquette: either you are infatuated with her or you can't stand her. Pierre Loti was able to plumb the depths of her heart and make Istanbul a unique heroine as much as a background for his works. It still has badly paved streets all tangled together without any apparent reason and cafés under hundred-year-old plane trees; one can savor their charm if one is sensitive to oriental refinement. Although it has been "made more commonplace day by day, alas! and profaned by everyone at present," Istanbul still has the same grandiose skyline as it did in Loti's day, and remains "the queen city of the East"[14] in search of an author…

Faruk Ersöz

14 *Constantinople in 1890*, p. 18.

Caïques in the Golden Horn.

CONSTANTINOPLE IN 1890

I am beginning this chapter with some uneasiness and great melancholy. When I was asked to write it, at first I wanted to decline; but that seemed a kind of treason to the Turkish nation, and here I am.

Now, in this instance I would be less capable than ever of writing an impersonal description with artistic detachment. Once more, those who consent to follow me will have to resign themselves to seeing things through my eyes: it is almost through my soul that they are going to perceive great Stamboul...

Ah, Stamboul! Of all the names that can still enchant me, this one remains the most magical. As soon as I hear it, a vision appears before me: very, very high in the air, far off at first in the blurry distance, there is the suggestion of something gigantic, an incomparable outline of the city. The sea is at its feet, a sea crossed by thousands of ships and small boats in perpetual motion; and from this sea rises the clamor of Babel, in all the tongues of the Levant; like a long, horizontal cloud, smoke floats over the mass of black ocean-liners and gilded caïques[1] on the multicolored crowds

---

[1] Long, narrow rowboat used on the Bosphorus; Loti will describe one later on.

shouting out their transactions, bargaining; the smoke ceaselessly covers everything with its veil. And there, above those buoys and coal dust, the immense city appears, as if suspended in air. Minarets as sharp as lances rise in the middle of the clear sky, dome upon dome piled up in terraces, like pyramids of stone bells: the motionless mosques, unchanged by the centuries-holy mosques whiter, perhaps, in former eras, when our Western vapors had not yet tarnished the surrounding air and only the sailing vessels of old came to anchor in their shade-but still the same, for centuries crowning Stamboul with the same gigantic cupolas, giving it this same unique skyline, more grandiose than any city on earth. They are the changeless past, these mosques; within their stones and marble lies the old Muslim spirit, which still reigns up there where they are. When someone arrives here from distant Marmara or Asia, they are the first things he sees emerging from the changing mists of the horizon; far above all the modern, petty agitation on the docks and ocean, they give one the thrill of old memories, the great mystical dream of Islam, the thought of Allah the terrible and the thought of death...

Long ago, at the foot of these dark mosques, I spent the most unforgettable times of my life; these mosques were the constant witnesses of my

The Mosque of the Mehmet the Conqueror (Fatih Cami).

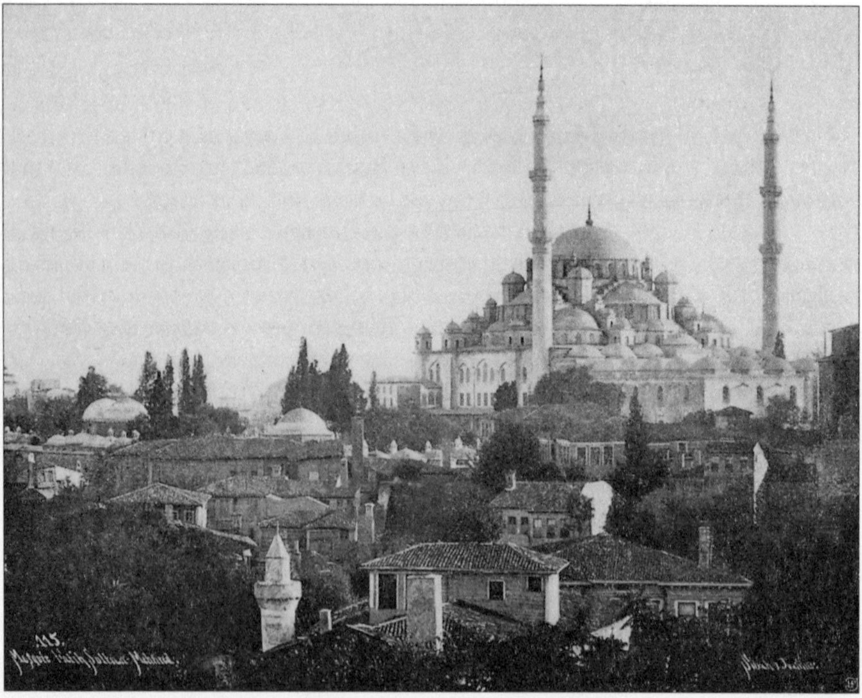

The Blue Mosque and the Egyptian Obelisk in the Hippodrome.

aimless rambles-while the delightful days of those times were so quickly fleeting. I could see the mosques everywhere, rounding off their great domes up above: now white and gloomy under the summer sun, when I would take shelter in the shade of the plane trees in some lonely old square; now vaguely black on a December midnight under the cold undecided moon, when my caïque glided secretly through sleeping Stamboul ever present, almost eternal around me-the passerby of one brief day, cast there by chance. A different sadness emanated from each of these mosques, a special reverence that hovered over the whole solemn neighborhood all around. Little by little, I came to love them strangely, the more I lived life like the Turks and grew increasingly attached to that proud, dreamy people; and my transitory soul of that time, full of anguished love, opened to the mysticism of the East.

Then, when I had to leave... oh! with what boundless melancholy did I see that outline of the city slowly fading into nothingness over the Sea of Marmara as we sailed away... When everything was blurry, almost gone, only the great domes and minarets still appeared over the cold fog of the sea; all that remained was the superb high skyline of Stamboul. And then that last image became the symbol of everything I was leaving behind me, everything

Saling from Marmara in the Golden Horn.

I missed so bitterly, my whole dear Turkish life ended forever: and the unique skyline was stamped inside my eyes in a way that can never be erased. Through the years of wandering that followed, all through my exiles, everywhere, over the far-off seas, in my nocturnal dreams, I would see the city of domes and spires outlined against the imaginary gray horizon of sleep, giving me the sad impression of a lost homeland every time. I could draw it from memory without a mistake; and in real life, every time I come back to it, I still feel an emotion, at once painful and delightful, that time has scarcely attenuated.

But I do not think the mirage of my personal memories is deluding me too much about the prestige of that view. It is undeniable and legendary: ordinary travelers, even those with no understanding whatsoever, feel a singular impression of *arrival* as soon as the imposing outline begins to appear in the distance. And as long as Stamboul-made more commonplace day by day, alas! and profaned by everyone at present-retains this first approach and those lines, it will still remain, despite everything, the queen city of the East.

Around Stamboul there is a group of other neighborhoods, other cities, and a series of palaces and mosques. Constantinople is made up of

The old city and the Bosphorus.

this whole: first Pera,[2] where the Christians live; then, along the Bosphorus, from Marmara to the Black Sea, an almost uninterrupted series of outlying districts. And all these parts of the whole communicate with each other through countless boats, legions of caïques. The city, scattered along the banks, scatters its colorful crowds over the sea-and the sea is covered with passersby, the sea is a place animated every day by these perpetual comings and goings.

Separate neighborhoods: in each, people of different races, religions and dress; these neighborhoods never resemble one another. No capital is more varied, nor more changeable from hour to hour, with its different skies, its winds and clouds-in this climate of burning summers and admirable light, but on the other hand, darkened winters, rains, snow suddenly covering thousands of dark roofs. And these streets, these squares, these suburbs of Constantinople-it seems to me they are almost mine, just as I belong to them. All those idlers spewed out by the Orient Express who throng the boulevards there today-I resent them walking around like intruders, profaning my cher-

2 Today's Beyoğlu.

ished domain without giving it the admiration and respect that old Stamboul still commands. Those neighborhoods, which they look at with banal astonishment-I know them as I know the neighborhoods of no other city in the world, I walked through them in the old days at all hours of the day or night, mingling with the life of the humblest of the humble as my whim then took me. So how could I talk about them in this book with the necessary objectivity? At every step I rediscover memories of youth and love. How could I judge them? I worship them!...

Before writing, I wanted to come back to Constantinople once again as an ordinary tourist myself, and take a more detached look at this city, where my only connection, alas! is now to dead people, where I have nothing else to do but visit graves.

And I went there from Rumania, in that spring of 1890, in the beautiful month of May, by the ancient rapid route through Ruschuk,[3] Varna and the Black Sea.

On the liner that was bringing me back on that Monday morning of May 12, 1890, all the passengers crowded the deck at dawn, on the lookout not to miss the entrance to the Bosphorus, a classic site with high ratings in the tourist guidebooks.

There are far more grandiose sites in the world, with more lush vegetation and higher mountains. Its intimate details are what create the unique

[3] Now Ruse, in Bulgaria, on the Danube.

Sirkeci Station, the last stop for trains from Europe.

The Dolmabahçe Palace.

charm of the Bosphorus-a real charm independent of my perception, since everyone who comes here feels it.

Now here is Çiragan, Dolmabahçe, the line of palaces white as snow, placed at the edge of the sea on marble docks. Then it becomes incomparably beautiful, for in the morning mist, the three cities appear all at once, three cities looking at each other: Scutari[4] to the left, in an amphitheater on the Asian bank; Pera to the right, a scaffolding of houses and palaces covering the whole European bank, and in the middle, on a point of ground jutting out between them, over a confused mass of boats and smoke, dominating the whole scene, the great domes and minarets of Stamboul!

On the heights of Pera, in the perfectly proper tourist hotel full of Englishmen where I am quite banally staying, my rented drawing room has a marvelous view over the Golden Horn, the tip of the Old Seraglio[5] and the little islands of Asia stretching out over infinities of blue sea. The immense vistas you can glimpse everywhere are one of the seductive features of this country. From any one of these three cities gathered here, you look out over the two others, with the sea beyond; wherever you live, you are always sure to see quasi-magical things outlined in the air over the foreground, over the roofs or trees. One's field of vision is wide and deep here as it is nowhere else in the world.

---

[4] Üsküdar.

[5] The old Harem is in Topkapı Palace, which its on Seraglio Point, where the Bosphorus meets the Golden Horn (Haliç).

Pera across the Golden Horn.

Main street of Pera.

Six o'clock in the evening, the same day. (You must forgive me: I spent my day in pilgrimages to cemeteries, in visits of memory to unexciting little corners of the city that hold an interest only for me.)

Sunset finds me on the banks of the Bosphorus in Tophane, sitting at an outdoor café-a habit of life in the East-watching the night fall and the world go by.

A jumbled, transitional place, this Tophane quay, a kind of huge crossroads, where absolutely different neighborhoods end up, carried by their broad streets.

On fine evenings like this, half the street is cluttered with rows of divans in red or multi-colored velvet; on them sit people smoking or dreaming. You sit there as in the pit of a huge theater, watching the great motion of Eastern life in front of you and the comings and goings of ships on the Bosphorus. Between the spectators of the sea, against the bluish background of the water and the Asian hills, a high mosque rises, with its complicated dome and its minarets with their perforated balconies. Its whites and reds are sharply set off against each other-two absolutely Turkish colors: together, on window-frames and panels, they decorate all the relatively modern buildings of Constantinople. Most mosques, palaces and the finest houses (if they are at all new) are painted in this half-and-half way; these shades go well with the blue of the distance or the water, and create a background themselves for the complex coloration of the passing crowds, with their countless red fezzes crowning every head. To these colors of the buildings, add the bright green of those large plaques bedecked with golden inscriptions that inevitably crown every doorway, every fountain. White, yellow, green striped with gold-these are the hues of the elegant mosque across the way, and also of the surrounding mosques, of that whole collection of constructions with oriental ornamentation standing out against the darkened sky, against the now twilight blue of the Bosphorus and Asia.

The rows of divans outside have been filling up indiscriminately with people of all the races and costumes of the Levant. Busy waiters run all over, carrying their microscopic cups of coffee, and raki, and candy, and glowing coals in small copper vases; the great easy promenade of evenings in the East is beginning, the hookahs are lighting up, and cigarettes of Virginia tobacco fill the air with their strong-smelling smoke. All kinds of people and vehicles are still going by on the street; handsome cavalrymen with a noble air going towards the Sultan's palaces or returning from them on their fine steeds; horse-rental men-Tophane is their headquarters-leading their saddled horses by the bridle; sailors of every nationality on land at the end of their day; peddlers ringing their little bells, or loudly hawking their cakes, their sherbets, their fruits...

A great clamor swells up in a crescendo from Galata,[6] whose eternally noisy main street comes to die at this crossroad; dulled though it is by the distance, it nonetheless reaches the dreamers here, on their red divans. Galata is the great Babel of the Levant. Till morning, all along the Bosphorus, a hellish clamor arises from this neighborhood...

Yeniçarşi also ends up here-the biggest of the steeply slanted streets that go up to Pera, the Christian quarter, perched up there over our heads. And on both sides of this street, under vine arbors, in front of the Turkish cafés crammed side by side filling up the sidewalk with their little stools and tables, hundreds of stevedores come to sit; they have worked all day carrying travelers' trunks, boxes and bales of merchandise up from the ships, the docks, the customs-houses. Happy with their evening's rest, they come in one after the other and order a hookah, these men whose job it is to replace trucks and wagons-unknown in Constantinople-with their broad shoulders and iron thighs.

Little by little, their crowd swells: soon they are all pressed against each other, dressed identically in brown monk's habits bizarrely braided with black and red, their vests wide open on muscular chests darkened by the sun. Their tight clusters extend over a tiered perspective, following the rapid rise of the street; the murmur of their conversations mixes in with that special

---

6 Now usually called Karaköy.

Tophane quay.

little gurgling sound coming from their countless hookahs; and the heady smoke fills the air more and more as night falls...

This whole little routine of the day's end has remained the same all through the many years I have known it: I have such a clear picture of what is happening at the same time in the different neighborhoods of the huge city!...

Down there, towards the north, continuing along the wide street that follows the sea, one comes to the quarters of the Sultan: an impenetrable palace, big walls around gardens, barracks, harems. There, all night brings is a great deal of tranquillity, under the avenues of acacias now utterly white with flowers.

Over our heads, up there on the heights looking down on our heads, cosmopolitan Pera is beginning to light up its big European shops with their window-displays copied from London or Paris; under the lights, its constant bustle of vehicles will continue, as it does in the West. Instead of calming the incessant agitation of life up there, the approach of evening will exacerbate it, under the gaslight.

Tourists rushing back from their daily excursions, eager to regain the reassuring fold before nightfall-the table d'hôte served English style, the street where they feel as if they're in Europe; extravagant outfits heavy-eyed

Turkish men smoking in front of a café.

Yüksekkaldırım, a steeply slanted street that goes up to Pera.

Levantine women venture to wear, women who would have been so pretty dressed like Greek, Armenian or Jewish women. And in this amusing jumble, with its oriental note sounded nonetheless by the many red fezzes in the crowd, by teams of stevedores coming up from the lower city in their many-colored embroidered costumes, or once again-as we are high over the sea-by distant vistas opening up between the banal houses several stories high: a bit of the dark blue Sea of Marmara, a bit of the Asian coast lost in the twilight...

Over there behind us, beyond that Pera hill looming over us, outlying districts peopled by Turks, Armenians or Jews sprinkle the slopes and valleys all along the Golden Horn, facing great Stamboul, which crowns the other bank and looks down on them. They communicate with each other above all by sea, using those light caïques, always in motion as long as a glimmer of light remains in the sky... Strange how the simple fact of being near things lost from view for years revives the memory one has of them: I haven't lived here for almost fifteen years, and I had almost forgotten how the evenings go by; yet all it takes is to be sitting dreamily in Constantinople, albeit in a different street quite far away, for me to remember everything with utter clarity, as if I had left yesterday... First the very Turkish district of Kassim-Pasha, with its old, very oriental little houses, small ancient shops, its little cafés shaded by plane trees. It was one of the neighborhoods I knew

Pera.

best back then, and I would walk through it every day. At this very moment I can see it suddenly animated with its special evening life. The wave of navy sailors has just spread through it, coming out of the arsenal or the big black battleships docked on the other side in the Golden Horn. Merry and full of laughter, walking around in groups holding hands, they fill the streets and squares. Instead of a sailor's cap, they wear a fez, and their color is red instead of blue: aside from that, they look like our sailors. Women who had been waiting for them (mothers and sisters, mind you) now mingle with them, draped in long white, blue or pink veils. Their officers stop there to smoke, too, in the humblest cafés, among men of the people. And in fact this very democratic mixing is a custom peculiar to Turkey: pashas, beys sitting in a café among poor people, chatting with them or explaining the news to them-and there is no risk of losing their dignity, for among Muslims one never gets drunk. Other outlying districts follow, looking more and more like villages as you progress toward the interior, and just afterwards, desert country begins, arid, roadless, and full of tombs; it has a sad charm.

The Golden Horn separates all the districts I have just talked about from great Stamboul, where a kind of religious silence is going to reign in the darkness.

And in the depths of this gulf enclosed by a city, in its profoundest depths, under the old cypresses and plane trees, the holy district of Eyüp, the

The Golden Horn and the arsenal.

Boatmen on the Golden Horn.

heart of Islam in Europe, hidden in a sort of small funereal wood, bordering the great cemeteries and surrounded by tombs, will fall sleep in terrifying silence, only interrupted from time to time by some psalmody coming from a mosque. In all the kiosks-stone booths of the dead-little night-lights will go on; as you walk along the dark avenues, you can see them shining through the latticed windows, like yellow eyes in the night.

Besides, all of great Stamboul will also fall asleep, almost as peaceful as in past centuries, while the racket of the West will start up in the districts of the bank abandoned to the infidels. Here and there, in the neighborhood of Saint Sophia, just a few shops will light up; a few cafés will project the glow of their lanterns outside; everywhere else in the immense city, there will be nothing but mysterious darkness and heavy sleep. It seems that this Golden Horn is not only an arm of the sea separating the two parts of Constantinople, but that it also puts two or three centuries between what is bustling about on one bank and falling asleep on the other...

While I am here, dreaming away in the middle of the street on this red divan, and peering through the smoke of the hookahs at the crowd walking about in the dim light, suddenly high up there in the air a first crown of fire lights up as a signal, around the pointed spire of a minaret in Tophane: the religious illuminations! Ramadan! ...I had forgotten that we were in this lunar month, when all working-class Turks turn night into day. So what was

I saying about the calm of Stamboul?... On the contrary, in a little while it will be noisier than Pera and Galata put together until morning comes-and I will go and mingle with this strange gaiety, with its crowds...

It is time to return to the hotel for dinner. Instead of walking directly up to Pera by Yeniçarsi, I am going to call over one those fellows in front of me leading saddled horses, and I'll take the longest way round, through the tumult of Galata, and then go up by Tarlabasi Road.

Galata by twilight and lantern-light! Crowds and noise. My horse skips around on the cobblestones, rather frightened, in the middle of the countless pedestrians, in the wave of red fezzes and monkish habits. Other horsemen go charging by, there is the continual coming and going of vehicles and heavy trolley cars preceded by runners blowing the trumpet. The smell of alcohol, absinthe and aniseed is in the air. Lights go on in the big, dangerous estaminets as they open; the big, fantastic alcazars illuminate their facades decked out with flags-places where they perform Italian pantomime next to places where female Hungarian orchestras play Strauss waltzes. The low-life spots are already crowded; people sitting in front of the cafés

Galata.

A street in Tophane.

obstruct the narrow street, jostled by the passing horses. The hubbub of conversations in every language, the confused noise of cymbals, bells, and bass drums is deafening. And now I am running rapidly through this overflowing crowd, calling out, for fun, "Bestur! Bestur!" (Watch out! watch out!), the cry of Turkish crowds, the equivalent of the "Balek! Balek!" of Arab crowds...

Back in the hotel up there, the banality of a table d'hôte. A tourist gentleman, recently spewed forth by the Orient Express, condescends to ask me for some practical information:

In the evening, there is nothing to do in Stamboul, right, sir?" (This is the cliché served up by all the hotel guides: nothing to do in Stamboul in the evening, and walking around there is dangerous.)

First I stare at him:

"Oh no, sir! Quite right, nothing at all in Stamboul. But here, in Pera, just next door, you have two or three delightful music-halls. Tell them to point them out to you..."

And after this dinner... Quick! a rented horse on which to flee...

I take Little Tarlabasi Road down through the beautiful starry night; then I ride through the middle of the celebration in Galata, and finally, leaving that noisy street, I stop at the water's edge, at the entrance to a bridge: its end is invisible, lost far off in the vague darkness. Here, everything brusquely changes, like the set of some extravaganza at the stage-manager's whistle. No more crowds, no light, no noise: before me lies a deep chasm of night and silence. An arm of the sea stretches out its calm, empty space between the deafening neighborhoods I have just traversed and another great, fantastic-looking city that appears beyond it-a black outline jagged with minarets and domes against the starry backdrop of the night. The skyline is so high that the cupolas of its mosques, distorted by the surrounding vapor, take on mountainous proportions. It is an evening of Ramadan. And so, at every story, the festooned balconies of those minarets are wreathed with shining rows of fire, and in the empty space between the stone spires rising right into the sky there are luminous inscriptions hanging from invisible wires, terrifying, like apocalyptic signs traced in the air with fire.

I can't wait to be over there; an attraction, the indescribable emotion of memory, makes me quicken my pace in the darkness of this endless bridge that leads, across the sound, to that terribly black city. As I draw near, the cupolas and minarets with their fiery crowns grow taller and taller. Now I am at their feet; I leave the unstable flooring of the bridge for the stones and potholes of the first dark square far under the superb mass of a mosque: I am in Stamboul!

I am going to turn my back on the new neighborhoods, the recently aligned boulevards, near Saint-Sophia and the Sublime Porte, now lit, alas! by gaslight, where horse-drawn Embassy carriages drive by, carrying adventurous travelers. I am riding towards Old Stamboul, going up through little streets as dark and mysterious as in years gone by, with as many yellow dogs lying curled into a ball on the street; they growl, and you stumble over them. Lord! Let's just hope some city father doesn't do away with them!... I feel a kind of sad pleasure, a drunkenness almost, plunging into this labyrinth where nobody knows me-but where I know everything, as if I were recalling a former life from a great distance...

It is a soft, marvelous May night. The darkness retains a transparence which enables one to find one's way, and above my wandering path, but very high, illuminating no more than the stars, the circles of fire hanging on the minarets of the mosques hover on every side, with their glowing inscriptions hanging in the air. The dark narrow streets I took suddenly end up in the huge Seraskierat Square, full of light, crowds, music, costumes. But I cross the square to penetrate more deeply into the heart of the city, into the exquisite, as yet unprofaned quarters of Süleymaniye and Sultan-Selim. Now

Roving dogs of Istanbul.

the darkness of mournful little streets, now lights and crowds. In the cafés, oriental music: sad violins moaning out heartbreaking melodies; bagpipes singing old airs in a bitter, plaintive voice. And men from the countryside, Asiatics, dance together in long lines, holding each other by the hand.

In that whole astonishing phenomenon of a Ramadan night in Stamboul, here is the image that charms me the most that evening: toward midnight, in a lonely street, quite simply a harem passing by... A very narrow street, very dark: above the high, barred houses, in a bit of the starry sky, one can see the minarets of Süleymaniye rising, gigantic black points-you would think they were diaphanous-bearing two or three dying fiery wreaths one over the other. - A great silence, and at first no one. Then a group comes on the scene, a group of five or six women, wearing noiseless Turkish slippers; blue, red, or pink phantoms, wrapped up to their eyes in those pieces of gilded silk lamé they make in Asia. Two eunuchs walk before them, armed with clubs, lighting their way with large ancient lanterns... It goes by, enchanted and charming; it goes further on, it disappears somewhere, to be

The Süleymaniye Mosque.

locked in some corner of a mysterious maze… And the darkness seems thicker now that the lights of their lanterns have disappeared, their shadows no longer dance on the old cobblestones and walls…

Tuesday, May 13, 1890. - I will relate this second day only from five o'clock on, and end it before nightfall.

So, at five o'clock, in a caïque, turning my back on the new parts of the city, I'm gliding up the Golden Horn to the outlying district of Eyüp.

(For those who don't know Constantinople, a caïque is a kind of long, slim one-seat canoe, bent like a crescent; you travel lying down. Hundreds of them can be found at all the docks, like gondolas in Venice.)

The Golden Horn grows more peaceful as we move away from the entrance, cluttered with ocean liners; the part of Stamboul I am passing now grows more and more ancient, dilapidated, dead: these are the very old neighborhoods. Little by little, life has withdrawn from them and gone elsewhere onto the other bank. Never before, however, had I found them so much like ruins invaded by trees, with black roofs almost vanishing under the fresh May greenery. And Eyüp is there at the end, touching the curtains of black cypresses, the great funerary woods.

A very sharp, almost cold wind is rising, as it does every evening when the sun goes down; little wavelets cover the whole surface of the water.

The holy district of Eyüp is still a privileged place for supreme contemplation and prayer. At the entrance to the exquisite avenue that runs alongside the holy tombs, I land on stone slabs that the centuries have turned green; the avenue sinks into the depths in front of me, gleaming white through a kind of sacred wood full of graves, white with the same greenish white that old marble takes on in the shade; it goes off to end up there at the impenetrable mosque whose dome can be vaguely distinguished under a clump of huge cypresses and plane trees. It is bordered on both sides by white marble kiosks with ornamental openings, full of catafalques and bodies, and by walls pierced with pointed arches through which one can make out the cemeteries; strange graves with faded gilding appear in the green forest-like darkness, mingling with tangles of grass, wild reeds, brambles.

Passersby are rare in this avenue of the dead: a few dervishes coming back from prayers, a few beggars going to squat over there at the doors of the mosque. This evening, there are three pretty little Turkish girls, from five to ten years old, skipping around in their striking green and red dresses. It is unsettling to see them playing gaily among the statues in this

Avenue leading to the Holy Mosque.

funerary shade. Yet I had never been here before during the splendor of May, and this new greenery, these flowers everywhere, are as out of place as the three little girls. Such infinitely melancholy places do not get any gayer in the spring-on the contrary! This gently shaded sky, these bunches of roses, the jasmine hanging over the walls-all that has produced the same ephemeral, highly deceptive smile for centuries in this season only adds to the impression one feels here of universal, irreparable nothingness.

Wednesday, May 14, 1890. - This morning at the French Embassy, around a big table full of yellow roses, there were at least thirty of us invited for lunch-all tourists!

In the past they were stopped by having to cross the Black Sea; but for two years now, with the new railroad ending at bottom of the Old Seraglio, it's frightful, this wave of idlers from all over Europe coming here to nose about everywhere.

And I have to smile when I remember the extremely charming wife of the Ambassador saying, as she glanced around her company at the long table with an incredibly subtle look: "Oh, as far as I'm concerned, you know, in the times we're living in, it hardly matters if there's one tourist more or less..." With no hint of a disagreeable implication for her guests, but pronounced with an indefinable, hardly perceptible nuance that turned this

The Golden Horn from the upper part of Eyüp.

View of Sirkeci.

simple little sentence into something infinitely amusing. Quite select, polite people of good society, these invited travelers. Just too many of them, becoming an invasion, and thus not decorative here to a painter's eye; that is all I blame them for-without meaning to imply, of course, anything more disagreeable than the Ambassador's wife did.

The same day, towards four o'clock, Stamboul in the rain. Since the morning, a storm has darkened the air, and the downpour is decidedly torrential.

As I leave the Sublime Porte, I take refuge in the labyrinth of the Grand Bazaar for the rest of the day: for Stamboul has its "bazaar," customary in the Orient; like a city within a city, surrounded by big walls, it shuts its thick gates at night.

It is dark and sad there today, under a sky full of water and those wooden roofs that cover all the little streets, and their oozing gutters; through a kind of steam, a twilight fog, one can see gilded fabrics gleaming, thousands of knick-knacks hanging from the stalls-and the crowds swarming: women veiled all in white, men in red fezzes. Thank God, this bazaar has hardly changed yet. In familiar nooks and crannies, I find the same dark little cafés with walls of old Persian faience tiles with strange flowers on them, cafés where they have served the same little, old cups for years. One can have the same dreams as in past years, looking through the open door at the Turkish crowd moving around in the fantastic half-light of the avenues. From the depths of these shadowy retreats, where people are smoking intoxicating Virginia tobacco, all that movement and noise seems, in the distance, like an enormous uproar of phantoms.

But alas, here are a few new attempts at European-style shops, complete with window-displays. And here are even a few groups of bewildered foreigners-tourists from the travel agencies, of course-walking by elbow to elbow, hurried along by shameless guides. (The British tourists are more confident: despite their air of walking through a conquered country, I really think I prefer them to the vulgarly sarcastic French, who complain about the unpaved streets, see only the few Paris articles displayed here and there in the bazaar, and tend to think that all those old, turbaned merchants squatting in the corners import their rugs from the Bon Marché or Louvre department stores.) And they'll all leave having *seen* Constantinople; they will all even complain about Muslim dishonesty, because they have been robbed, pillaged (their fate by right) by vulgar guides and interpreters-who are Greeks, Armenians, Jews, Maltese, whatever you like, but never Turks. Turkish workers become boatmen, day laborers or stevedores, but never stoop to ply the servile trade of exploiting foreigners.

I linger, bargaining over old silver trinkets, while the light fades outside and the rain is still falling. Its business over, the bazaar is emptying, growing more and more desolate: the shops close all along the very old, covered alleys, both merchants and customers leave, and gray darkness descends on this labyrinth. At night, it will be nothing but a black desert.

Yes, I must go. I get back on the wretched hired horse that was waiting for me at one of the gates of this bazaar soaked from the day's rain, and I ride toward Pera.

The rain is ending; but the sky remains gray, the old roofs are still streaming. As you ride down toward the Golden Horn through the narrow streets, you splash through puddles, and mud spatters out all around. The city has suddenly taken on the look of winter-the look, in fact, that I knew best; it is dear to me in the most intimate way. Here is where my impressions become quite personal once again: Stamboul is ugly and sad on this kind of evening, and yet this is how I love it most. I return reluctantly, very slowly, despite the water still falling from a thousand gutters on the wet roofs. Oh, how I plunge back right into my past, on this rainy, chilly evening…

When I get back to the hotel, still without haste despite my soaking clothes, I find a note from His Excellency the Grand Vizier, informing me that His Majesty the Sultan wishes to invite me to come to Yildiz Palace this evening to see the illuminations for the Kadir gecesi.[7] "A carriage and a tchaush[8] will come to pick you up," he tells me.

---

7 Twenty-sixth night of the month of Ramadan, a great Muslim celebration.
8 Palace guard serving as special messenger.

The interior of the Grand Bazaar.

Merchants in the Grand Bazaar.

Wooden houses in old Stamboul.

About three quarters of an hour afterwards, almost late, after dining perfunctorily and feverishly washing and dressing for the occasion, I am riding rapidly toward Yildiz in an open landau escorted by a galloping tchaush, cutting through the crowds of Pera. The sky has cleared: the stars are shining. The marvelous Ramadan illuminations are lighting up all over; when a vista opens up between the banal houses, it seems an enchantment.

Yildiz Palace is far away, almost out in the country, on the other side of Stamboul, to which we are turning our backs in our rapid ride. The Bosphorus, which we can also glimpse from time to time, and Scutari beyond it, are illuminated like the European coast; the enchantment stretches out on all sides to the utmost limits of vision.

Now before us, running in the opposite direction, there is a wave of people, a human mass rushing madly, with half-naked men galloping and shouting. I can make out the sinister call in the distance: *Yangun vâr!*

Fire! There's a fire! With so many wooden houses, it happens all the time here. A whole neighborhood is burning over there, hurling a great red glow into the sky, adding an unexpected light to the celebration. Those things being dragged along so quickly with a heavy sound are pumps yoked to panic-stricken men running as fast as they can; a pump gets caught in the wheels of my carriage... Shouts, violent pushing... But they recognize the palace tchaush, they get out of the way and we get through...

Now, suburban avenues, wide, straight, almost empty, where we hit our racing speed once again.

Firemen.

Then, in front of us, a great white and green glow, not of fire but of fireworks: the Yildiz Gardens. We ride through the gates: now, suddenly, both crowd and noise are gone; we are galloping along empty, silent lanes, profusely lit, lined with myriad fires making garlands and festoons. Nothing but white flames in white globes amid the greenery; no coloring here on the ground, whereas the sky is all starry with blue and red rockets, and striped with fire raining down in every color.

The garden paths, still empty, go uphill; it is getting lighter and lighter, a white light, while one side of the horizon remains bloodied by the red of the fire. Another gate. Then battalions of horsemen and foot soldiers block our way, in tight ranks; they are all carrying torches or lanterns, as if for some gigantic torchlight parade. Hundreds of officers too, for the most part wearing the oriental dolman with long floating sleeves. Oh, what a beautiful, imposing army!

These thousands of men, so motionless, seem absorbed in religious contemplation in the middle of this strange, dazzling light, under this rain of fire whose changing colors streak through the night sky.

The Yıldız Palace and the Imperial Mosque.

The tchaush who is leading me has the passwords, and the ranks open before us. He conducts me to the second floor, in a wing of the palace: empty salons where it is astonishingly bright-the brightness of inside lamps and outside illuminations: their immense glow comes through the wide-open windows. The woodwork and furniture are white and gold; everything is luminous and white. There is some particular form of silence which gives one the feeling of that mass of men out there, almost mute, almost holding their breath, oppressed by the presence of the sovereign. And admirable religious music is coming in from outside: a choir of extremely fresh, limpid men's voices, a psalmody of extraordinarily high notes, with something unnatural, almost extraterrestrial about them...

An aide-de-camp greets me in these salons. "The sultan is still in the imperial mosque, where those exquisite chants are coming from." But the prayer is ending, and if I go over to a window I will soon see His Majesty coming out.

That mosque appears about fifty paces away from me, slightly below my window. It is sparklingly fresh and white, highly scalloped with arabesques, Alhambra style. Illuminated from without and within, it seems as transparent as a fine cutting of alabaster, and that music coming from the mosque turns it into something unreal: it is like the showpiece of the immense fireworks burning all over tonight. Around its strangely luminous dome appear the avenues and gardens through which I came, with their myriads of white globes. Clouds of fireworks blur all the distances before me, jumbling all the perspectives-already complicated because I am looking from a height. Mysteriously suspended in the air, a gigantic transparency displays a brilliant Arabic inscription against a night-colored background. With all the dazzling phantasmagoria that scramble our vision, it is impossible to guess how far away this aerial inscription is located: it seems large and distant like a sign from heaven; it presides over this festival of light; this inscription is what gives the festival its Muslim, sacred character. And still further on, one can glimpse fragments of real distances: little shining objects with a special form are set in a vague black expanse that must be the Bosphorus; they are boats illuminated up to the tip of their masts...

Directly below me, the superb army, still motionless and rapt in prayer, is following in spirit the chants inside the luminous mosque across the way. At this moment it seems as if the soul of Islam is concentrated in that white sanctuary. Oh, the chants, monotonous as magical incantations, vibrating under that cupola with such beautiful, rare, sonority! Voices of children or angels, it is hard to say. There is something extremely Oriental in them, too, sustaining ultra-high notes without strain, while retaining the unchangeable freshness of oboes. The chant is long, long, repeated again and again, it comforts us like a lullaby, and yet it expresses human nothingness with infinite sadness; the vertigo of great abysses takes hold of us.

....

Selamlık at Yıldız, ceremony on the occasion of Friday prayer.

Meanwhile the sultan is going to come out. A slight, attentive shudder passes through the troops. A landau yoked to parade horses-rearing as they trot, prancing on their hind legs-parks in front of the marble steps of the mosque, covered with red carpets; at the same time, thirty-odd servants come running, each carrying one of those enormous white silk lanterns, one yard high, which have been an obligatory part of the etiquette for the caliphs' nocturnal outings through the ages. Under the cupola, the religious choir is singing more rapidly and loudly, in its final exaltation...

Allah! Here is the sultan! Palace, gardens and sky blaze with a brighter fire. The cannon thunders like a great storm, and all the troops, bowing to the ground, shout together, in thousands of voices: "Allah! Allah!" in a long, deep, roar...

To cross the hundred yards that separate the mosque from the doors of the palace, the landau has gone into a racing gallop, carrying the sovereign; behind him, other magnificent carriages are galloping too, bringing the veiled princesses who have been at the service; the panicked servants run around, shaking their big white lanterns, and the troops close ranks again over this procession in a clicking of arms. It is over.

Following an aide-de-camp, I walk through salons and corridors with walls and columns in light colors, slightly gilded. Here at Yildiz, there is great sobriety in the ornamentation, as if to say, enough luxury! The sovereign, who possesses enchanting palaces in peerless sites along the Bosphorus, prefers the relative simplicity of this residence for work and rest; he himself had it built next to a great shady park.

Here I am at last in a sort of immense court antechamber, equally simple: its only luxury is the magnificent carpets that muffle the sound of footsteps. This evening it is peopled with generals, aides-de-camp from each branch of the military, in full dress uniform, some wearing a long straight tunic, the others the oriental dolman with big floating sleeves, some wearing a red fez, the others a black astrakhan hat. They do look very much the warrior; their assembly, at this threshold of the imperial apartments, is more imposing than any magnificent display-and among them, there is the heroic figure of Osman Pasha Ghazi, the proud defender of Plevna.[9] Everyone is standing, speaking in hushed tones, which seems to indicate that the sovereign is near.

Indeed, in a small lateral salon into which I am led by the grand-master of ceremonies, His Majesty the sultan is sitting on a couch, alone. He is wearing a general's uniform covered by a brown military cape, with no outward sign to distinguish him from the officers of his army.

I have not had the honor of seeing him for a very long time. As I

---

[9] Today's Pleven, in Bulgaria. Osman "the Victorious" led the Turks who valiantly defended it in 1877 for four months against the Russian Army.

make my bow to give the court salute, I suddenly think, rather sadly, of a first irregular interview, which the sovereign cannot possibly remember...

It was on the Bosphorus almost fifteen years ago, on the day of his accession to the throne-one of those clear sunny mornings which, seen through the filter of memory, seem to us more luminous than mornings today. The big imperial caïques with golden prows had come to Seraglio Point to take him to Dolmabahçe Palace. It was very early, the sea was free of crowds-in fact of any guard around the convoy-and my own caïque, which was going heedlessly by, had run afoul of his, through the clumsiness of our boatmen: and then the young prince, who would soon be the supreme Caliph, had mechanically given me one of those distracted glances which do not see, his black eyes seeming to plunge anxiously into future things...

Alas, that day's future has become today's past, and that image, called up by memory, suddenly makes me measure the gulf of dead time that already separates both of us from that morning full of sun and the bloom of youth.

The sultan's welcome for his guests has always been exquisitely gracious, combining distinguished simplicity and natural grace. The moments of that evening in which I had the honor of chatting with the sovereign will always be unforgettable-in the rather strange calm of that soberly furnished little salon, quite ordinary in fact, but with its threshold so gloriously guarded by those military leaders talking in a low voice, and its windows open to the far-off tumult of the celebrating city, against a sky lit up by fireworks and the glow of a fire.

Sure of being understood and forgiven with the most charming indulgence, I dared to express all my melancholy regret in seeing the old things disappear, in seeing great Stamboul opening up and being transformed.

But I cut short my artist's complaint; in a chat with a sovereign, a passing traveler like me cannot allow himself to say what I would have liked to add, even during the most gracious of audiences:

What will soon become of poor, great Turkey-so proud in the era when the strength of nations came from faith, sublime dreams and noble personal valor-as she is inevitably dragged down to our universal modern banality, faced with the thousand little petty, practical, utilitarian things that she once was able to disdain? What will she be like, especially when her sons no longer have the faith?

While expressing my terribly deep attachment for this brave people, I was nevertheless tempted to suggest my saddened concern, to try and learn if the caliph could glimpse some mysterious dawning of a new era that my weaker vision could not yet perceive beyond the frightful transitions of the present.

....

The Dolmabahçe Palace seen from Asian coast.

Main Gate of the Dolmabahçe Palace.

Seraglio point, the last promontory of Europe.

Thursday, May 15, 1890. - It is morning, very early morning, fresh and pure.

I awake, not in my official lodging in Pera, but in the middle of Stamboul, in one of those ordinary little inns where you sleep on the floor, fully dressed, on white mattresses.

Having left the imperial palace late last night, I threw off my gala dress when I went by the hotel and quickly came here, on the other bank of the Golden Horn, to mix once again with the nocturnal celebration of the streets. Then, as the last fires of Ramadan went out on the minarets, I walked at random into the nearest lodging to sleep.

No clock rings out at night in these quarters of Stamboul, and when I wake up I worry about the time, as one of His Majesty's aides-de-camp is to pick me up over there in my official apartment to show me the treasures of the sultans.

I walk out the door of the inn; outside, I find the enchantment of living, I get drunk on merely breathing. These old, little streets, where no one goes by, light up joyfully in the eternal sun as if for some festival of youth that will never end. Oh, the rare purity of this oriental May morning, the utterly new, vivifying freshness of this air, this light!

Having gone back down near the Golden Horn, I come to this

square lined with ancient plane trees; the Valide mosque[10] towers over it on one side, with its tall, gray mass, its minarets and its Arabic lacework. On the other sides, there are vine arbors, little cafés, tiny shops for barbers and merchants selling babouches[11] -very old and very oriental, all this, and utterly unchanged: it could have been Ispahan or Baghdad.

The early May morning is even more delightful on this square than in the streets. The rising sun gilds the mosque, gilds the plane trees from underneath; there is a white mist in the air that is like the virginal veil of the day. The little Turkish cafés are beginning to open, and two or three fellows are already being shaved by the barbers outside, under the trees.

It is clearly very early, and I have time to stop here before going back to Pera. I sit down under the vine-covered trellis and order a coffee with those little hot sweets they sell here in the morning to ordinary working people, and all this seems better to me than the most refined breakfast. One seems to feel, rising in oneself, that renewal of life which is shining forth everywhere outside, rejuvenating the ancient things all around.

About two hours later, toward eight o'clock, a carriage is taking me back to Stamboul again, dressed quite differently, in the company of an aide-de-camp of His Majesty; and, in a solemn, deserted neighborhood, where grass grows between the cobblestones, our coachman stops before a frightful wall, like the ones surrounding medieval fortresses.

These walls enclose a small corner of the Earth that is absolutely special, unique, the furthermost tip of eastern Europe, a promontory jutting out towards neighboring Asia, and what is more, it was the residence of the caliphs for centuries-a place of incomparable splendor. Along with the holy district of Eyüp, this is the most exquisite place in Constantinople: it is the Old Seraglio, the Harem; the name alone is enough to stir up a world of dreams...

A citadel gate is opened for us in the walls, and then, as soon as we pass through it, the delightful melancholy of inner things is revealed to us, the dead past takes hold of us and envelops us in its shroud.

First silence and shade. Empty, desolate courtyards, where the grass of abandoned places grows between the stone slabs, where century-old trees are still living, contemporaries of the magnificent sultans of days gone by: dark cypresses tall as towers, plane trees that have taken on unheard-of forms, all hollowed out by time and just managing to prop themselves up on monstrous strips of bark, bowed down like old men.

---

[10] Yeni Valide Camii, built between 1597 and l660. At one end of Eminönü square, near what is now the Karaköy bridge. Valide means "mother": Sultan Mehmet IV's mother finished construction of the mosque.

[11] Turkish slippers.

Marketplace and the Yeni Valide Mosque in Eminönü.

Cook in the street.

Gate to the second courtyard of the Topkapı Palace.

Then come galleries, colonnades in the ancient Turkish style; the veranda, still painted with strange frescoes, where the great Süleyman condescended to receive the ambassadors of the kings of Europe... And this place, luckily, is not open to profane visitors, has not yet become a vulgar outing for tourists; behind its high, thick walls, it retains a bit of mysterious peace, it is indelibly stamped with the sadness of dead splendor.

As we walk through the first courtyards, we leave impenetrable gardens behind us on our right, through which one can glimpse old kiosks with closed windows: residences of imperial widows, of aged princesses who come to end their days here in an austere retreat, in the middle of one of the most admirable sites in the world.

The last part of this walled-in place we have come to is full of sun, dazzling in the tranquil light: the final tip of the Old Seraglio[12] -and of Europe. It is a solitary esplanade, very high, very white, looking out over the far-off blues of the sea, and Asia. The bright morning sun is flooding the deep space out there, where cities, little islands, and mountains are outlined in light shades over the motionless sheet of the Sea of Marmara.

Around us are ancient constructions, equally white, which contain the rarest, most precious things Turkey possesses:

---

[12] The site of Topkapi Palace. See note 5, above.

View of the Topkapı Palace from the sea.

First the kiosk, forbidden to infidels, where the Prophet's robe is conserved in a protective cloth embroidered with jewels;

Then the Baghdad kiosk, its inner walls completely covered with the Persian faience tiles of long ago, priceless today: the branches of red flowers were made with coral, liquefied by a process now forgotten, and spread on like paint;

Then the imperial Treasury, also very white under its layers of whitewash, and barred like a prison. In a little while they will open its iron doors for me.

And finally a palace, uninhabited but meticulously maintained, where we will go in and sit down. The white marble steps lead us to the salons on the ground floor, which must have been furnished in the middle of the last century in the European taste of that time. They are in Louis XV style, to which an imperceptible trace of oriental strangeness lends a special charm. White and gold woodwork, old-cherry or old-lilac lampas silk with white flowers; nothing but light colors, softened by time. Great Sèvres and Chinese vases, a small number of objects, but all ancient and rare. A great deal of space, air, light; a tranquil symmetry in the arrangement of things-things, one senses, accustomed to immobility, and neglect.

And here, in this rather sumptuous solitude, sitting on delightfully paled pink armchairs, in front of the opened, wide windows, we have the splendid view of this last promontory of Europe that charmed the sultans of yesteryear. To our left and far down below our feet, the Bosphorus rolls out before us, furrowed by ships and caïques; the whiteness of the marble docks are reflected in it; the whiteness of the new imperial residences, Dolmabahçe and Çiragan Palaces, is reflected upside down in long, pale streaks; the series of palaces and mosques stretches out magnificently on its banks. Facing us, there is Asia, still bluish in a remnant of morning mist; there is Scutari, with its domes and minarets, with its enormous cemetery, its forest of dark cypress. To the right, the infinite reaches of the Sea of Marmara; far-off ocean liners are sailing there, lost in all that diaphanous blue, little gray silhouettes, trailing smoke...

How well chosen this place was, to dominate, to watch over all of Turkey, resting proudly on two parts of the world! And today what peace here and what melancholic splendor in this utter isolation from the agitation of modern life, in this great silence of abandonment, under the bright, mournful sun!...

When the guardian of the Treasures-an old man with a white beard-gets ready to open the iron door for us with his big keys, twenty sworn-in guards stand in ranks, ten to the left, ten to the right on either side of this entrance: obligatory etiquette.

We walk through the middle of their double file and we go into rather dark rooms, where they all follow us.

Never was the cave of Ali Baba filled with such riches! For eight centuries the rarest jewels and the most astonishing marvels of art have been amassed here. As our eyes, now rested from the outside sun, become accus-

Rumelihisarı on the European shore of the Bosphorus.

Summer residence of the French Embassy at Tarabya.

tomed to the dim light inside, diamonds begin to sparkle everywhere. Shelves house a profusion of priceless, ageless things classified by kind. Weapons from all eras, from Genghis Khan to Mehmet; silver and gold arms laden with jewels. Collections of golden caskets of all sizes and styles, some covered with rubies, others with diamonds, others with sapphires; some of them even carved out of one emerald as big as an ostrich egg. Coffee services, flagons, ewers in exquisite, ancient forms. And fairy-tale fabrics; saddles, harnesses, parade saddle-cloths in silver and gold brocade, embroidered and re-embroidered with flowers in precious stones; extremely wide thrones, made to sit on cross-legged: this one all in rubies and fine pearls which lend a pink glow to the whole thing, that one entirely covered in emeralds and gleaming with a green reflection, as if it were streaming with sea-water.

In the last room, behind glass, a horrifying, motionless company is waiting for us: twenty-eight macabre life-size dolls, standing straight, lined up in military rank and touching elbows. They are wearing that tall, pear-shaped turban that has no longer been in use for a century, and is only seen now on catafalques of great dead personages, in the half-light of funerary kiosks, or sculpted on tombs-so often that for me this turban is absolutely linked to the idea of death. Up to the beginning of this century, whenever a sultan

The Galata Bridge.

died, a doll was brought here in the full regalia of the dead sovereign, with his marvelous weapons in its belt, his turban with its magnificent spray of gems on its head; and it remained thus forever, covered with these eternally lost riches. The succession of twenty-eight sultans who reigned from the conquest of Constantinople to the end of the eighteenth century have their dummies standing in this room in full dress; slowly, the sumptuous, somber assembly grew, as new funerary dolls came one by one to take their place in the line of old dolls who had been waiting there for hundreds of years, sure of seeing them come. And they are elbow to elbow now, all these phantoms who reigned centuries apart; time has brought them together in the same pitiful non-being.

Their long robes are made of the strangest brocades, with large, mysterious designs and shades of color faded by the passage of time; with their broad pommels made out of one precious stone, priceless daggers rust away in the silk belts, despite all the care lavished upon them. Even the huge sprays of diamonds seem to flash more gently now, shining with a tired, yellow gleam.

And this unheard-of luxury, sprinkled with dust, is sad to behold. Fabulously magnificent, these dolls in their high headdresses (objects of so much human desire, guarded there behind double iron doors, useless and dangerous) see the seasons, years, reigns, revolutions, centuries go by in the same immobility and the same silence, and without light as soon as the sun sets... Each one has its name, written like a banal word on a faded label-illustrious, terrible names: Murad the Conqueror, Süleyman the Magnificent, Mohammed and Mehmet... I think these dolls are giving me the most terrifying lesson of fragility and nothingness...

At the "ladder" of the Old Seraglio a large palace caïque is waiting for us, eight pairs of oars, and we step down into it and stretch out on cushions: this way of traveling half-reclining, with your eyes at the level of the water over which you glide, is peculiar to Turkey.

The rowers all wear the traditional white silk gauze shirt, open over their tanned chests: impassive, darkened by the sun, they seem to be bronze figures with porcelain teeth.

The calm Bosphorus sparkles in the burning light.

We give a wide berth to ocean liners, to smoke-to everything that dirties and clutters up the sea across from the Golden Horn.

In two or three spots, at Dolmabahçe on the European bank, at Belerbey on the Asian bank, we land on immaculately white marble docks, in front of deserted palaces with white, gilded wrought-iron gates. This is the unique charm of these royal residences, their snowy whiteness at the very edge of the blue water.

Imperial Post Office.

Inside these uninhabited palaces, whose guardians open their doors for us, a great deal of magnificence: forests of columns in every color, tangles of chandeliers and candelabra, extremely complicated ceilings in the oriental style, spangled brocades and Bursa silks. But no one in these stately rooms, in the middle of all this luxury-so fresh, kept up with so much care. The sovereign and his court do not even come here any more.

It is close to noon when we go back to Yildiz Palace, after this rapid visit to the other imperial residences.

In Yildiz, an impression of extreme calm, of serenity and silence. We are still in Ramadan, a period of prayer, of retreats, and, in the house of His Majesty the Sultan still more than anywhere else, fasting is rigorously observed: it may only be broken after sundown during this holy month. A lunch is served only for me, as one not subject to Muslim law; but now I feel quite embarrassed sitting down to table in this palace where no one is eating. For the first time in my life, to lunch seems almost an impropriety to me, a Western vulgarity.

Besides, I have much better things to do. On the gilded pages of a pad that an interpreter has brought me, I again have the privilege of communicating a bit of my written thought to the sovereign, invisible today, but whose proximity can be sensed. And I marvel that despite the thousands of consuming occupations of royal life, His Majesty should be so familiar with all that touches upon literature and art.

Artillery Barracks at Taksim.

The open windows let in a flood of light, and silence; the rays of the May sun dance over the white walls, over the bright brocades of the furniture. A view of flowering gardens in the foreground, then of deep distances: again those charming vistas of the sea and of Asia one has from anywhere in this terraced city, the outpost balcony of Europe.

The imperial mosque is here, too, nearby, displaying the ornamental apertures of its dome. And, while smoking the most exquisite cigarettes of Virginia tobacco, I chat about last night's religious chants with His Excellence the Grand Vizier, who can become, when he wishes, the most courteous and refined of Frenchmen.

"Go over to a window," he says, "And listen to the incomparable voice that is going to sing out a prayer in a moment."

Indeed, in the middle of the tranquil silence outside, suddenly the voice arises, delightfully resonant; it has the bite of an oboe and the celestial purity of a church organ; with a kind of inexpressive detachment, as if in sleep and in a dream, it rings out the Muslim prayer to the four corners of the blue sky... And then an intense impression of Islam comes back to me, making me shudder to the depths of my being; in this gay, bright salon that might easily be somewhere else, in any château in France, little by little I had lost that impression: it is infinitely melancholy to me, both lulling and distressing, an impression I never been able to define.

Students of the Artillery School.

Still more beautiful than that golden voice, vibrating today with youth and power, but which will disappear tomorrow, still more beautiful is the almost immortal chant that, for centuries, five times a day, hovers over the Turkish cities and land. It symbolizes a whole religion, a calm, proud, mysticism; it is the lamentation and the call sent to the heavens above by those brothers of the Orient who are better than we are at retaining the old, consoling dreams, who still walk along with closed eyes so as not to see the dusty abyss, and who fall asleep inside magnificent mirages... As long as that prayer continues to make heads bow around the mosques, Turkey will always have the same superb soldiers, just as indifferent to the thought of dying…

ırches by, slim and noble under his naval uniform all decked out with crosses, ·ning his pretty, intelligent face to the onlookers: he charms everyone. The ople in the tourists' salon do not know him, and a few women in hats flowing like a May garden lean out the window to get a look at him, asking: who he? He is little prince Burban-Eddin, the last of His Majesty's sons.

Almost noon. All eyes are turned toward the palace. People look at eir watches-traveler's watches, never in agreement, set to all the different mes of Europe. The troops adjust their position and raise their head; a udder ripples through the ranks, heralding the approach of their sovereign. he brass bands explode into sound, striking up the imperial hymn. And up ere, in the high balcony of the white minaret, under the golden crescent, e muezzin has just appeared,[18] so small under the sky and the sun-the uezzin who is going to chant the holy prayer...

Noon! Suddenly the bands stop playing, in the middle of a phrase, s if struck dumb; there is a silence, unexpected, sudden, striking, as if ppressed by something slightly terrible, and the troops freeze in breathless nmobility. Then the three cries: Allah! Allah! Allah!-a formidable soldier's hout from five thousand powerful chests-shake the inert, warm air... And in he renewed silence after that enormous roar, the sovereign rides by.

He is in a carriage; with Osman Pasha, the illustrious hero of Plevna, n front of him;[19] he goes by quickly, while every head is bowed.

And from on high, from that sky of white fire, the chant of the nuezzin descends-the ancient, Oriental call. The marvelous voice, chosen out of all other voices, dominates earthly sounds, covers the military orders and the vague murmur of so many thousands of men; it is fresh, facile and nfinite-somewhat strange as well, with its melancholy oboe-like timbre. Its rapid, wild flights take off and descend lightly above human heads, transmitting a mystical impression of Islam, even to the alien unbelievers assembled here to see the show...

The Caliph gets down from his carriage and walks up the marble stairs on the red carpet. The Oriental robes and dark turbans spaced out along the steps bow down to the ground. The last notes of the celestial voice, plaintive now, die out up above-and it's over. The Caliph has gone by. We begin to breathe again, to talk freely, after that religious shock, and conversations start up again in the cosmopolitan groups in the pavilion, while handsome military horses parade by on a tight rein, white, with gold harnesses... The moment was short, fleeting; but all the same, in the midst of this splendid production, we could still feel the thrill of being touched, however lightly, by one of those special beings called emperors or kings, who personify great nations.

---

18 The crier who, from the minaret of the mosque, call the faithful to prayer.

19 See *Constantinople in 1890*, Note 9, p. 44.

Selamlık at Yıldız, ceremony on the occasion of Friday prayer.

A SULTAN PASSES BY

I am looking out of a window in one of the pavilions of Yildiz Palace, the usual residence of His Majesty the Sultan.

And the window, needless to say, frames a great, rather special setting, quite unique, which immediately yields a precise indication of the time and place.

First of all, in a powdering of dust, in the blazing noontime sun of June, under a sky pale with heat, an unbelievably white mosque-but an elegant new mosque, though built in the purest ancient style. This mosque seems to have the refinements of modern Islam, something like new Gothic churches in which the quest for the archaic harmonizes with perfected techniques. Almost too pretty, with its high portico crowned with Arabic trefoils, with the very delicate cut of its windows, the grace of its minaret covered with ornaments like stalagmites and crowned with a sparkling gold crescent.

Everything immediately surrounding it is new and well-ordered too, sanded, raked; the trees are young, the lawns well-mowed and dotted with baskets of flowers, with all the care usually lavished on a prince's residence.

Behind the white lace-work mosque in the middle of the picture-its main, essential subject-one can sense the great marvels of yesteryear. The Bosphorus and the silhouette of Scutari in Asia[13] are piled up in the distances arranged in superimposed levels that show we are looking from on high. Then comes that incomparable vision, Seraglio Point,[14] thrusting out into the waters of Sea of Marmara, with the minarets, cupolas and cypresses of Stamboul-all merely suggested by bluish grays, drenched in sunlight, in the midst of the sparkling sea; all barely recognizable under a veil of luminous dust, taking up very little space in the background, behind the beautiful mosque in the foreground. Just as in certain early Flemish or Italian paintings, tiny houses and palaces are piled up under the arms or against the shoulders of the figures in the middle... But what a marvel, the cape of Stamboul with Saint-Sophia and the Old Seraglio: the mere suggestion of its presence beneath the modern décor is enough to call up the memory of the magnificent past and inspire our respect.

The roads, paths and twisting avenues near the imperial mosque are full of marching soldiers, approaching to the sound of military music. And these troops are increasingly condensing around the white sunlit walls of the sanctuary; we can sense that something solemn is going to happen inside. One can see them passing each other, zigzagging, like the endless parades of theatrical extravaganzas; cavalry flags, black banners embroidered with silver, and red lance pennons pass in front of each other again and again in a cloud of continuously rising dust; the great bright brasses of the bands sparkle in the sun; so do the tall Chinese hats decorated with pony tails. Chimes and fanfares sound, the air is full of the deep, strange notes of Turkish trumpets. And still more soldiers arrive, massing together according to a pre-determined plan, with perfect regularity, suddenly stopping at their position in the parade. The closest, drawing up in serried ranks directly beneath us against the walls of the kiosk, are Arnouts[15] from the north of the empire and Zouaves from Tripolitania[16] in green turbans-their costume, attitude and whole formation as magnificent as their individual beauty.

Now they are all in place, motionless; they seem lost in reverence, for the holy hour of noon is approaching, and soon the mosque will hold the

[13] See *Constantinople in 1890*, Note 4, p. 21.
[14] See *Constantinople in 1890*, Note 5, p. 21.
[15] Albanians.
[16] Western Libya, along the Mediterranean coast.

ceremony for which they are all assembled, the "selamlik," the prayer: His Majesty the Sultan will be there in person.[17]

Reverence does not yet seem the order of the day in room where I stand; diplomats are chatting with ambassado discussing political questions among themselves.

No one is particularly reverential in the neighboring roo crowded, full of women above all, tourists of different European na the request of the embassies, the grandmaster of ceremonies has a them come see the selamlik parades. And an aide-de-camp, th pleasant Mehmet-Bey, with his long, flowing Circassian sleeves, does hastens to guide the lovely tourists to appropriate places. ..."His Ma going by this very spot, beneath our windows-on horseback, or in A question that preoccupies many spectators; it is impossible to rep this space of two or three hundred yards between the palace and t the Sultan usually finds it simplest to take a carriage, followed by his b led by the bridle. Now this is visually regrettable, for His Majesty lo sive on a horse and besides, on horseback he corresponds better to of a Caliph than by riding in a landau like any ordinary western sove

But the time is drawing near. The marble stairway of the m just been hastily covered with a precious red carpet on which the step, and strange Asiatic groups have lined up on either side of their long green, yellow or orange robes are striking against the sn of the walls-dark-haired heads with a somber gaze, wearing wide priests delegated from over there, from Mecca or Baghdad. The Cal gious empire extends to such distant lands, and they bring to this ized Orient the wild, charming note of ancient times…

Troops are lined up in double ranks along the sanded avenu dignitaries of all kinds are beginning to arrive for prayers-officers es generals, marshals, all the heads of the valiant Turkish army; but hardly glance at them, waiting as they are to see the Sultan pass by

And now, in elegant closed carriages, the princesses of the i family; but their dresses and faces are hidden in a cloud of silk chiff

The sun is blazing. In the brilliant white salons, on the brillia mosque, in the distances blurred by shimmering dust, a powerful beaming, and it seems that the heat is made heavier still by the presence thousands of armed men all massed here, not speaking and holding their

One by one, the persons of rank invited to the selamlik conti arrive; the imperial princes, the older ones with their aides-de-cam youngest, children in military dress, with their tutors. A ravishing little

[17] The Selamlık is actually the public procession of the Sultan to the mosque f the great Friday prayer ceremony.

On the Galata Bridge.

MOTH

In my family home-my private dwelling, which is like a small corner of the old East-on a dull, hazy spring evening, between the dark, half-closed curtains, a sad gleam of twilight slips in, making a long ray through the darkened air.

From the folds of a red velvet wall-hanging embroidered with archaic gold patterns, something extremely little escapes, as if attracted to that dying streak of day-and once there, it begins to flit around wildly: a gray moth, barely visible, a winged wisp of straw. It has probably just hatched in the springtime, so very pale this year.

The season before, while I was roaming the China seas, it had been some kind of horrible little worm, gnawing away unseen at the weft and warp of the precious velvet in the constant darkness and silence of this apartment.

And today, a whole new life was intoxicating that atom, and this little space seemed big to it, and this semi-darkness seemed like light. It was its hour of youth, its hour of exuberance and its hour of love, the goal and crowning moment of its whole inferior larval existence. Quick, quick, delirious with existence, it was fluttering its wings of silky dust, describing gay, capricious little curves…

As I walked by, I automatically flicked it to the ground with my finger. Then, on the floor, on the purple red of an oriental rug, I could again make out the little body I had knocked down, shaken by its final tremors-and, out of pity, to send this nothing back into the nothingness of everything without further suffering, I stepped on its microscopic death-throes…

Afterwards, I remained pensive for a moment... What was it that this brought to mind? Years ago, somewhere else, something a bit like that-a kind of agitation, a similar gray fluttering-had briefly aroused in me a melancholy feeling of the same kind, but sharper... So where had I seen that?

Oh yes! ...In Constantinople, on a dull April evening like this one, on the wooden bridge that connects Stamboul to Pera!.[20] ...I was passing by, at the end of a hazy spring day, like today. All the beggars who frequent this spot were at their stations; along the handrail, a line of the usual faces: the crippled, the blind, idiots covered with sores. Among others, a pathetic child of four or five with his shriveled hands and sick eyes, motionless in the same spot day after day, sagging under his rags, sitting on the curb, apathetic and slow as a larva. And behind him, his mother squatted, an old woman displaying the red stumps of two legs cut off at the knees.

People were passing by, busy or idling: horsemen, carriages, the men in red fezzes, the fine carriages of the harems. And, behind the crowds, Stamboul magnificently piled up its domes in the sad twilight sky.

In a voice that was almost gentle, the legless woman called her little boy, saying in Turkish: "Come put your coat on, Mahmud! Come quickly, the wind's cooling off!"

He got up obediently and walked over to her. His coat was an old, small, sordid grayish burnoose with blurry stripes, hooded in the Oriental style. His mother handed him this rag, and he held out his skinny arms ending in crooked hands.

But suddenly, before putting his arm into the second sleeve, he escaped, in a sudden burst of mischief, and began running and running,

---

20 See *Constantinople in 1890*, Note 2, p. 19.

circling madly around the passersby, playing at flapping the sleeves of his burnoose like wings, in the cold wind that was rising...

A bit of that eternal youth-so fleeting-a bit of that playful childishness at the beginning of life common to both men and beasts alike had happened to awake in him. As with everyone else, there must have been healthy people in his ancestry who had felt surges of physical joy, the simple joy of existing and moving. So something of those departed ancestors had come briefly alive again in his frail, atrophied flesh.

I looked at him amazed, as I had always seen him inert; and his poor, brief spurt of gaiety, his joyful flitting about, the fluttering of his grayish burnoose in the cold wind and the pale light, stirred in me an indefinable feeling of infinite sadness.

The legless mother was worried because of the horses and carriages; she kept calling him, getting angry, trying to drag herself over to grab him. But he kept on spinning around the indifferent groups passing by; madly spinning around, like the gray evening moths...

However, he returned to squat at his wretched post; he took up his collapsed position again and did not move an inch. It was over as suddenly as it had begun.

Something crueler than the flick of the finger I'd given the moth had just knocked down this little person, already capable of thought: worry about shelter and an evening meal; the awareness of being wretched and so different from others, of having dead hands and of being an outcast.

With bowed head, he was now staring at the ground with a sneaky, wicked expression, blinking his eyes full of evil...

The association in my memory between him and the moth is even more intimate than I have been able to say...

Pier of Arnavutköy at the Bosphorus.

OLD BOAT, OLD BOATMAN

Out of all the little boats waiting by the dock in Therapia, ready to cross over to the other bank of the Bosphorus, we had to pick one. Most of them were pretty, colorfully painted, with fine velvet cushions, each with its young, muscular oarsman.

Only one of them, the nearest, the one whose turn it was, looked like a poor relative compared to the others; no velvet on the cushions, but calico slip-covers in little multi-colored scraps; a boat quite clean, however-well taken care of, but so old, patched together, and steered by an ancient boatman dressed so wretchedly! Almost roughly, I waved it off and called the next one, all fresh and gilded, over to the dock.

But when it got out of the way to make room for my boat, I saw how carefully and ingeniously the calico scraps had been patched together and mended: no doubt the work of some old woman, this old man's wife, to try to make the worn old boat look a little more presentable and not repel customers too much. Above all, I met the boatman's eyes, a look full of suppressed reproach, resignation and distress...

And then my heart was wrung by terrible pity; it darkened my day. I promised myself I would return the next day and pick this man out of all of them, compliment him on his good taste and his modest improvements, even take him every time I crossed over.

But I could not find him-not the next day, nor the days after that. Perhaps this is truly puerile, but of all the bad things I've done in my life, none has left me with more remorse than the affront I gave that poor old man and his little calico slip-covers so laboriously arranged, humbly trimmed with red braid...

THE GREEN MOSQUE

The main entrance of the Green Mosque.

To the French Ambassador,
Monsieur Paul Cambon

I

Bursa, May 20, 1894.

Sitting in the morning shade, the imams of the Green Mosque were beginning their dream of the day. The first hours of the newborn sun had just brought them together in their usual spot, at the edge of the holy terrace, under hundred-year-old plane trees. Behind them rose the marble façade of the mosque. And at their feet, before their eyes lost in contemplation, the city of Bursa, drenched in greenery, went sloping gently down to the far-off abyss of the plains.

The imams of the Green Mosque were dreaming in the shade. The fresh leaves of the plane trees spread a cool dome over their motionless turbans. There were few sounds to trouble their wandering thoughts: the twittering of birds, the music of running waters, and happy voices of small children in the distance. Half hidden in the trees, the city below was sending them the faintest murmur of its tranquil life, muffled under so much foliage.

The terrace in front of the mosque where the imams were dreaming was like a peristyle that already had a religious function; it formed the outside sanctuary. It was surrounded by a low wall covered with little mayflowers; the entry was a gate open to all. In addition to the venerable plane trees that sheltered the imams, there was also a big, dark cypress and a white kiosk-one of those stone booths for the dead-with slender arches; a fountain was gushing out of it...

When I entered this place of continuous peace for the first time with my travel companion, we had only been in Bursa since the previous evening, brought here by the French Ambassador.

The house in which the Ambassador had offered his charming hospitality was located half way up the mountain, outside the city, almost in the

Bursa, a view from the citadel.

fields, between Bursa and the village of Çekirge. A brand new Oriental house, hardly finished, with its ceilings and doors still in white pine; down-below, a vestibule floored with faience tiles; up above, our rooms that looked out on infinite distances; and a large living room with whitewashed walls, on which they had quickly tacked silk and gold-threaded embroideries shaped like the doors of a mosque.

Since we had arrived by carriage very late on a moonless night, we had not been able to glimpse anything of the delightful old city. And this morning, with our windows open to the bright sun, we had immediately been struck with wonder to see everything appear; we'd had the impression of plunging into the ancient days of Islam, of seeing a spring of yesteryear in a calm, verdant Eden. Then we had gone out into the luminous countryside; eager to get to know this Green Mosque, we had rented one of those little carriages that are parked at most crossroads under the big trees. The Turkish trap had an odd gondola-like shape, crudely painted all over with all sorts of patterns and flowers; it had poor suspension and hung low to the ground; its curved roof had shining copper and pearl decorations on it; the coachman wore a red vest with gold braid; the white horse, gaudily dyed with henna, had necklaces, pendants and little bells hanging around his neck. It all bespoke an archaic, naïve East, still a bit childish, reveling in the pleasure of lively hues.

We encountered many similar carriages on the way. They trotted by gaily, sparkling with painted designs, in the midst of the green springtime,

The house of the French consul.

under the arches of fresh leaves, along the banks of high weeds dotted with red poppies. And in those carriages, there was a constant diversity of dress: men in embroidered and re-embroidered vests, women draped in long veils of gold-spangled silk that allowed only their lovely painted eyes to be seen. Beneath our feet stretched the immense plain, with trees billowing out to infinity like the curling of a green wool rug. And Bursa was before us, clinging to the side of Mount Olympus, which towered over everything with its summit still striped with snow-a city half buried in the tangled branches, sensed rather than perceived, a sort of forest the color of Spring. Here and there, the domes of the mosques, and the white minarets and black cypresses emerged from its depths. We also passed slow-moving carts drawn by gray water-buffalo, their heads crowned by blue pearls, and white oxen with their foreheads reddened by henna. And groups of peasants obstructed the road, carrying extravagant loads of mulberry branches for the silkworms that have toiled for centuries unawares, weaving the famous Bursa cloth.

We were finally inside the city, and had begun driving noisily over the hard cobblestones. The little wooden houses on both sides of the street passed by unevenly, never falling into line. Hanging far out, the upper stories were supported by voluted corbels, usually all askew on the lower stories following unpredictable whims, but the better to turn towards the beautiful landscape, the infinite plains, or a barred window through which women peer out. There were small, naively decorated shops housing odd little crafts, plied without undue haste, using techniques of the past. We became increasingly aware of a retreat into those good old days here, into times less difficult for craftsmen and the poor. We felt how simple life had remained here, and how contemplative: countless dreamers were sitting in the shade of the trees, in the doorways of cafédjis or barbershops, in front of a hookah, a microscopic cup of coffee, or a simple glass of water cooled by a bit of snow from Olympus. Trees, trees everywhere, streets completely covered by ancient vine-arbors and brand new vines. At crossroads now and again we had little glimpses of distances bathed in green twilight, like underbrush in the distance, and the charming medley of colorful old Turkish costumes, untouched by our own dull fashions. A large number of mosques, all sheltered under gigantic, ageless plane trees with monstrous trunks, still admirably green in their extreme old age. And so many gushing fountains, flowing down from the high snows in little trickles or in lovely fan-shaped sprays. This whole shady city was riddled with flowing water, which then fell and gathered in the plains down below.

And so many graves everywhere! Along the streets and public squares, the dead mixing with the living; the funerary kiosks, the greening tombs in the darkness of their huge cypresses... But none of this created any horror or fear, in the midst of this people of believers: it seemed as if the invisible people lying underground were simply pursuing the tranquil dream of their life, the same dream, with just a bit more mystery, a bit more silence and a bit more night....

Bursa kept flying by before our eyes as we drove on in our little painted carriage. After riding for half an hour, we came to a ravine, wide and deep. A torrential stream was flowing through it, under a mass of trees. Bridges crossed over it, ancient, massive bridges built on huge Byzantine arches-and, since these bridges were of unequal width, all along the parapets the Turks had built little suspended houses in order to enjoy the strange site: these were inhabited bridges. Unlike Arab cities, whose impenetrable dwellings are always windowless, buried in whitewash, the painted wooden cities of Turkey look out on every side through thousands of openings, masked only by thin metal lattices in accordance with the Muslim rule.

When we had finally gone through the city, our carriage stopped under the plane trees near the Green Mosque. Already under the spell, indeed almost reverential, we walked through the little door and into the holy courtyard. Then we saw the imams sitting at the very edge of their terrace, silhouetted against the deep distances they were contemplating. Their white and green turbans had hardly turned in our direction before they plunged back into their dream, leaving us to contemplate as well.

The Mosque towered over us, white and calm. Despite their immaculate whiteness, the marble walls, buckling slightly under the weight of centuries and earthquakes, immediately gave us the impression of far-away times. Grass was growing here and there, making a green border between the foundations and the busy doves, who made their nests in holes in the

The façade of the Green Mosque.

wall and were flying back and forth all around. The high door had mysterious designs on it, and was crowned with something like a series of falling stalactites; the windows were framed by fine Alhambra lace. Despite the highly complicated details, the main lines of the whole structure remained restful, simple. The man who created the Green Mosque and built it here before these deep perspectives five centuries ago, as a forward balcony over this country of trees-that man was a great master of dreams.

Invaded by grass that is never disturbed, the white marble steps were all dotted with red poppies today: the Turks feel the charm of ruins, and wild flowers take over the most splendid human achievements. Besides, if they never repair anything, it is so as not to thwart the will of Allah: everything falls, everything comes to an end...

The imams sitting in the shade had understood our desire to enter the sanctuary: they had sent us a young man who had been dreaming there, lying beside them.

He was a poor boy: his trade was to rent babouches to people visiting this holy place. He had come humbly, to put these Turkish slippers on our feet and open the doors to this serene mosque for us.

At first, all we could feel was an impression of coolness, of delightful semi-darkness, of supreme peace; then, slowly, we became immersed in the special charm of this place.

In the middle, a fountain gushed out of a pure white basin. On the big walls, rare faience tiles-the technique of coloring them has been lost for three hundred years-alternated with the whiteness of the marble. The great tiled loggia of the sultans of old appeared high above the entrance, and on either side, on a level with the marble pavement, similar loggias opened up for the imams. They were lined with precious tiles representing unimaginable flowers, framed and bordered in every conceivable turquoise blue, from the cool turquoise color of the clear sky to a dying turquoise fading into strange greens.

At the back of the mosque shone the Mihrab, which is, as everyone knows, the very holy portico facing Mecca: the faithful turn to it as they pray. An extremely tall, majestic masterpiece of ancient art, it was made entirely of colored tiles; its flowers, arabesques and raised inscriptions full of infinite curlicues; its pointed arch, with thousands of smaller arcs in it, overlaid with stalactites, like slow crystallizations in caverns. And, above it all, crowning this mass of complications, a series of large polychrome trefoils stood out against the white marble of the walls.

And still, both here and outside, for all its prodigious accumulation of details, the mosque itself remained simple, designed with superior artistry

The tomb of Sultan Mehmet I, (Green Mausoleum).

to be restful to the eye. The calm emanating from it may have come, perhaps, from the total absence of living forms: none of those painful images, often superb but always all too human, that decorate our churches. Even the flowers had something rigid that transformed them; a geometric regularity was everywhere, the impersonal, the abstract, the inexistent; the arrangement of things and their pure outline, already suggesting the approach and peacefulness of a kind of inorganic beyond-immaterial, eternal.

We had wanted to visit the tomb of Sultan Mehmet I, the founder of this mosque. It was nearby, on a slightly warmer esplanade, and we had to go under the old plane trees once again, and walk up a few stone steps.

Here at this tomb one finds the real Green Mosque-a name that is nonetheless so appropriate for all of this holy place because of the admirable greenness of the surroundings and the green shade cast by the plane trees here above the steps.

An octagonal funerary kiosk, crowned with a dome and decorated on the outside with little verdigris tiles imitating lizard scales.

Inside, an enchantment! in shades of emerald and ocean. Faience tiles like the ones on the outside, but embroidered with delicate golden arabesques, and in the middle of each face of the green octagon, a polychrome rose window-one of those rose windows so complicated and simple at the same time, in a Persian shawl design narrowing to a point ending in a kind of fleur-de-lis. Small stained glass windows high up next to the dome, finely crafted like pieces of jewelry, let a changing light pass through as if filtered through precious stones. The floor is overlaid with the thickness of ancient rugs, on which we walk soundlessly, in slippers. And in the center of the kiosk, the catafalque, the monumental, slanted, coffin-shaped catafalque, surmounted by an old-fashioned turban and covered with a veil from Mecca in pale gooseberry-colored silk with dull silver inscriptions. A wonder of Oriental art, this great, sad thing, richly adorned with silver, before a background the color of seawater...

Then the slipper-rental man brought us back into the first courtyard, near the silent imams, suggesting that we, too, sit at the edge of the terrace and enjoy the incomparable view of far-off distances.

As we approached, the imams touched their right hands to their lips and then to their foreheads as a gesture of friendly greeting, inviting us to sit next to them on a red carpet. And thus our acquaintance and mutual sympathy had begun.

The imams' favorite spot is a modest, extremely old wooden platform supported by the trunk of a big cypress tree; one walks up three steps, all cracked by the sun. Its floor is quite worm-eaten. Built at the very edge of the terrace, it just reaches the top of the little surrounding wall, enabling even a sitting person to enjoy the whole marvelous panorama down below.

Coffee and hookahs are brought to us once we are seated, and the little slipper-rental man sits in the circle with us, too, for poor as he may be, the imams accept him into their company. First of all, working people here are all more or less refined by prayer; and then, Turkey is the home of real equality-equality in contemplation and dreaming. The Turks do have a faith, a powerful clergy, a theocracy and a caliph; but that does not prevent rich and poor, common laborers and the most learned dervishes, from shaking hands, sitting side by side in the humblest little cafés, and talking to one another. We are utterly ignorant of their very real fraternity-we Westerners, promoters of fine egalitarian theories that end up in an explosive mix after having led us into the shameful, stupid dupery of a financial aristocracy.

The conversation on the imams' terrace makes us forget the passage of time: it is very slow, full of long silences, made up above all of pleasant formulas, smiles, and calm gestures pointing to the great horizons stretching out beneath our feet.

First the city of Bursa, birthplace of the Osmanlis,[21] fans out on the slopes of Mount Olympus at the same altitude as ours. The city dives deep, almost drowns, vanishes into the leaves, under the branches of all the trees, so cool in this beautiful month of May. The Turks call it *The City of Five Hundred Mosques*; and indeed, floating on the green wave are above all the holy cupolas, the white spires of the minarets, and then the great black tears of the cypresses, saying that the dead are everywhere, the Osmanlis of old are still there, sleeping under the footsteps of their pious sons…

The city does not descend at all regularly and evenly into the plains. We see ledges here and there, stretches of terrain advancing like prows, bearing mosques emerging from the greenness, and more visible houses. And, at the edge of these escarpments, more terraces stretch out before us, places where other dreamers like us sit contemplating the distances.

All velvety with trees-poplars, mulberry trees, oaks-the plains below lead away, bluer and bluer, to a ring of very distant light purple mountains that touch the pure sky. And behind us, this mosque with its great marble walls also seems to be contemplating something through its festooned windows, spreading its mystical calm about our heads…

A bit to the side of the sacred enclosure, there is a group of men. Sitting or lying down, with their elbows on the little surrounding wall, all of them remain silent as they gaze into the depths of the green gulf: ordinary country

21 Members of the Turkish dynasty founded by Osman I, ca. 1300.

The Mihrab of the Green Mausoleum.

people, shepherds or bandits. Tall and blond, superb, their eyes shadowed, their light moustaches standing out in their suntanned faces, they are wearing short red or blue vests that reveal broad cashmere waist-bands rolled around their supple waists. Their sleeves, cut in Tartar style, hang freely from their shoulders, a little like wings: their pants with a thousand folds are cut off at the knee, displaying, in Anatolian fashion, a sinewy calf above the tight gaiters. The very model of the dreamer warrior: they have been or will be those soldiers of the faith, admirable under fire, who make up Turkey's armies and make them so strong.

A healthy summer heat already hangs in the dry, sweet air. The perfume of the countless roses in the gardens rises up to us, mingled with the balsamic odors of the cypress trees.

"Are there many panoramas in your country as beautiful as this one?" asks one of the green turbans with a smile. From the tone of his question, one can tell he does not think it possible.

What an elevated, wise vision of life these people have! Considering the things of this world as transitory; trusting in God and praying; creating very few needs, very few worries, and enjoying the least briefly possible that which is true beauty here on earth: springtime, limpid mornings, and golden evenings.

And already there is a mutual sympathy between us; they have no doubt understood that we are almost Orientals, for the tormented side of our character escapes them...

Bursa is dozing gently under the heat of noon as we go through it again to return to our Ambassador's house. And many people are kneeling with their hands clasped and their heads raised in prayer.

The Muradiye Mosque.

II

Among all the peaceful, dreamy places that make up the city of Bursa, one is particularly exquisite: the hedged funerary landscape around the Muradiye mosque. There, under cypresses as high as towers, under century-old plane trees as high as Nubian baobabs, are the kiosks that serve as the last resting place for several past sultans. Like lianas, rosebushes run from one tree to another, flowering in amazing profusion along the pathways invaded by wild grass. Everywhere water gushes forth from the old fountains; every branch has a bird's nest on it. This is a shady, hedged, and above all rose-filled landscape. For once, there are no distant vistas: one can only guess at the plains below, without seeing them; one is enclosed under a green arch, between green walls that make the peacefulness here more inviolable than elsewhere, and sadder, too.

And, out of all those very old kiosks-which a dreamy imam has opened for us, one after the other-the most charming is the kiosk of Prince Mustafa (1472).[22]

The interior is covered with the most admirable Persian faience tiles. On a bluish background, there are small repeating patterns of imaginary flowers in archaic, rare designs; flowers in two blues, lapis and turquoise, alternate with coral flowers in raised enamel. A faience frieze runs above this magical tapestry; it has a black background with white religious inscriptions on it punctuated with bunches of pink flowers. And today we are still searching for the secret of that coloring, lost for three centuries.

Since the prince asked that his grave be covered by a lawn and watered by the heavens, his faithful successors left an opening in the arch of this priceless kiosk for the rain to fall through. The catafalque of white marble in the form of a huge open coffin has been filled with reddish earth where pale, sickly grasses grow between the marvelous tiled walls.

In the evening, we are drawn back to our friends of the morning, to the beautiful Green Mosque.

A small funeral procession was arriving at the same time: a young man on a stretcher carried on the shoulders of other young men, meditative and grave. The body, rigid forever, was covered by embroidered fabrics that outlined its form, and we could not see his face, hidden beneath a veil. Nothing lugubriously sad, but rather a serene, sweet melancholy in this death scene, this procession-so young, brightly, colorfully costumed, passing under the plane trees on a spring evening, surrounded by all those flowers...

We slowed down to let them pass.

For a moment they set down the litter on the steps of the mosque. Then, without being called, the imams rose slowly, in their priestly robes, and came to stand around the dead man and pray.

And then, when the prayers were all recited and the burial procession had left, they turned to us with kindly smiles, inviting us to come up to the platform once again, and share the evening dream with them.

Just as he had this morning, a nearby cafedji brought in coffee, hookahs and primitive little sorbets cooled with real snow from up there; then, seeing that we wished to pay for the snack in our turn, "Oh!" they said jokingly, "You are mussafirs (foreigners); your money would not be accepted in our city," and the cafedji, who was in cahoots with them, refused our offers. Yet they were almost poor, and a few coins still meant something to them; but their refusal had such distinguished grace that all we could do was give in and smile in our turn.

---

22 He actually died in 1552. The mosque of Murad II near the village of Çekirge was built at the same time as the Green Mosque; the nearby cemetery holds the tombs of twelve members of the imperial family.

Truly, those who have only met the Turks in Constantinople or in other ports already deflowered by contact with us do not know them; to appreciate their open hospitality, their perfect courtesy, their tact-and their scrupulous honesty-one must go to the less traveled cities of the interior.

"Where did they take that young man?" I asked.

"Up there," they said, still smiling, as if there were nothing definitive or dark about that destruction of life, "*He went up there to sleep on the mountain.*"

Guardians of venerable old rites in the most exquisite of sanctuaries, the imams had never felt the need to travel very much. One of them, who did not even know Stamboul, questioned me about what the Bosphorus looked like.

The group of handsome proud warriors with blond mustaches was sitting motionless at the edge of the terrace, as they had been this morning.

"What are those men doing?" I asked. "What are they waiting for, in the same spot, for so many hours?"

"Why, they are *looking*, of course!" he answered.

This motive for the lengthy immobility of these men seemed natural and sufficient to him.

Four delightfully pretty little girls between six and eight noiselessly opened the gate and walked into the courtyard. Their long dresses had the brilliant colors of flowers; little painted veils of white muslin over their henna-tinted hair gave them funny little coifs. They were holding green June bugs tied by threads; each of them had a rose with a sprig of jasmine on her forehead and cherries tucked over their ears. Their black eyes already held all the mystery and charm of Oriental women.

On the sad stone slabs, next to the grave imams, they took off their shoes, heaped their clogs and babouches into a pile, and began skipping over it, singing a slow song.

And the imams of the Green Mosque, turning their eyes away from contemplations of the infinite, now enjoyed watching the little girls jump; in the shade of the old plane trees, against the background of the white marble of the mosque, they were as fresh and striking as poppies or daisies-little flowers of Turkey themselves...

It was the time when swifts whirled joyfully in the air, making their loud cries, the most golden time of the evening. Down below, at the depths of the horizon, mists-already orange and pink-were melting into the furthest summits; the mountains seemed to be delicate, frozen clouds, and the clouds seemed slightly fantastic mountains whose outlines were slowly changing, disturbed by imperceptible breezes.

Muradiye Street.

We took our leave of the imams of the Green Mosque and the slipper-rental man, shaking hands with all of them this time, as with friends. We were going up to a place called Bunarbashi (Head of the Springs) before nightfall-to higher parts, at the very top of that wood which is a town.

And our carriage began to climb extremely steep slopes, between houses whose upper stories hung out over the narrow streets. All along the road there were many venerable little mosques, more or less in ruins, many cypresses and tombs. And, still climbing the slopes of Olympus, we could see deeper and deeper vistas of the plains below.

Bunarbashi, a shady plateau, where very fine grass grows under the cover of ancient willow-trees with huge branches and trunks twisted like the bodies of monsters. Here and there, large cypresses with graves turning green beneath them, and naturally, many gurgling springs, a lot of transparent, cold water, recently escaped from snowy summits. It is a spot walled in by trees, where there are no scenic views, a place that induces melancholy contemplation. Yet children play there, children with beautiful eyes full of the joy of life. And women go walking there, draped in veils dyed in delightful, delicate flower shades.

The Şehzade Mosque.

We stop there for a moment in front of a little isolated café. Silent men are sitting near us, in the charming glow of their Oriental dress. They are listening to the gurgle of the cool springs; they are staring in front of them at the closed-in meadow and the nearby graves: under the stones, in the roots of the cypresses, no doubt, the dead continue, though more vaguely, the same dream as theirs.

We go back down in the pink twilight, following the Byzantine walls that once surrounded Bursa; the ruins are still imposing, of almost Cyclopean breadth. As the view is still prettier from the top of the walls, little wooden houses are perched on them, just as down below they perch on the parapets of the old bridges.

From this descending path we have a strange, glowing view of the entire old Turkish city at sunset: it seems part of a landslide, tumbling down under the greenery. Resting on odd rocks in a kind of promontory, a few mosques thrust almost whole out of the branches and soar upwards, extremely majestic. Out there, bluish forests appear far in the distance, peopled with deer; beneath our feet, the plains of green mulberry trees, and over our heads, ancient, snow-white Olympus, the land of all the nice dancing bears that mountain people trot through the towns to the sound of the tom-tom to amuse all the little children in Turkey.

The crickets are chirping on this fine starry night, the fireflies carry their sparks through the air while we go to sleep in the house of our

The Ulu Mosque.

Ambassador, in our little rooms of fresh wood, vaguely hearing the sound of running water and the trilling song of the nightingales in the midst of the silent countryside.

The Green Mosque seen from Setbaşı.

III

Wednesday, May 30.

Sitting in the shade of their plane trees, the imams of the Green Mosque had gone back to yesterday's dream as soon as morning came.

Three new figures had joined them today. First an old imam straight out of Oriental tales, so old, so old that when he was motionless he seemed hardly alive. Long white beard, long white robe. A personage all in white on the red carpet, he was sitting next to the others, continuing a dream he had begun almost a century ago. Then a black in a green turban, who was returning from the holy cities, and a *Maghribi*, an Algerian Arab.

Off to one side, the group of handsome warriors in embroidered vests, and under the arches of the white kiosk, the four little girls with cherry earrings: in all, our whole tranquil little entourage from the day before.

Renewed greetings with the imams, still friendlier this morning. To honor us further, they seated us on either side of the old man, and he smilingly gave us his hand as he welcomed us. The Green Mosque, too, seemed more charming to us, its lines more harmonious; an ever-increasing peace emanated from its marble façade and marble steps, invaded by red poppies and the grasses of the field.

The black told us he was from western Sudan, but no longer remembered his country, as he had been brought to Bursa as a small child. The Algerian related that he had come here after a pilgrimage to Mecca-without quite knowing why, a nomadic whim perhaps: but now he missed his country, which he had left two years ago, and longed to return. It happened that H. de V., my traveling companion as he was in Morocco years ago, had lived in his village, knew his tribe, his chief. This moved the exile to tears. Then a conversation began between them in Arabic while I spoke Turkish with the imams, and coffee, hookahs and little sorbets were brought in. A delightful shade was coming down from the plane trees, it was exquisite to breathe the wind that blew over this hanging terrace that looked out over vast horizons; under the white kiosk, the gushing fountain cooled the air; it even seemed that coolness was issuing from the nearby sanctuary, from that whole mass of marble and tile that makes up the Green Mosque.

We left them as we had yesterday, at the warm hour of noon, promising to come by that evening-our last evening-to bid them farewell.

This time our carriage went through the long bazaar to cross Bursa; it was cooler in that place, in the semi-darkness of those arches. And we watched the displays going by, their colors standing out in the obscurity, the bright rugs, the many-colored fabrics-especially the famous silk gauze of Bursa, fogs of pink or blue, impalpable, and striped, it seemed, by lines of fallen snowflakes.

Here and there the vaults of the bazaar were colored by great naïve paintings. They represented ideal holy cities, all mosques and tombs, where sailing vessels shaped like ancient barks were docked on a China-blue sea. Then we went through the craftsmen's quarter, makers of copper pitchers, embroidered harnesses, door-knockers, trays and little decorated boxes. Here and there, in the middle of the shops, food merchants displayed their little sober, tidy kitchens, decorated with flowers. Very little meat; boiled grains, porridges, dairy products, pink slices of watermelon. And robust market-porters, laborers, came to buy, in doll-dishes, little bits of those things which are enough to maintain their superb muscles-so much is sobriety habitual and hereditary in Turkey. No wine, of course, no fermented liquor; nothing but lemonades, kept cool under blocks of snow from Olympus.

As we go by, we have glimpses of the side streets: under vines hanging from ancient trellises, under gigantic plane trees, the little cafés where working people happily take their rest, in the gentle drunkenness of the hookahs. They are content with a few hours of work for slim wages, so modest are their needs and desires. After all, one can always buy a pretty embroidered jacket that lasts a few seasons and pay for one's seat on a bench in the summer shade or the winter sun. Then, when life declines, faith is there to drive away the terror of death...

As the sun was sinking that evening, we came back to the Green Mosque to take a last farewell of our friends.

The old imam with a snow-white beard was sitting next to them, as he had been this morning, in the folds of his white robe. And we resumed our conversation-we who apparently belonged to such distant worlds and, one might say, to different centuries.

And they pointed out to us the principal mosques among so many domes that rose from the greenery, and named their founders, almost invariably buried in their vicinity:

"This is the mosque where Sultan Osman is sleeping, and in the other one, Sultan Murad..."

....

"Are there men," interrupted the old man all in white, "Are there men as old as I am in your country?"

"I don't know," I answered. "How old are you, father?"

"About ninety-five."

"Oh! Yes, in that case, there are."

Silence.

"And are there men who reach a hundred, in your country?"

....

A little spiral of smoke appeared, in the infinite green of the plain, in the sea of trees stretching out beneath our feet, smoke spiraling rapidly toward us. The old man pointed it out to me with a gesture emphasized by his ample white robe, but his wink and slightly sarcastic smile meant:

"And are you familiar with that thing... the thing that comes from your country?"

Yes, unfortunately I was familiar with it, and I, too, began to smile at his delicate mockery. The train! The little narrow railroad that has connected Bursa to one of the ports of the Sea of Marmara for the past year.

"In your country, if we were standing on a height as we are now, we would see many of them go by, I suppose?"

"I'm afraid we would, father..."

"Here, we only have one, oh! Just one! ...But," he added, "*Yetişir!*

Yetişir!" (That's enough! that's enough!) That is indeed enough. In fact I think it is too much, but I don't dare express this idea to him.

....

We turn around as we hear the gate of the high terrace opening behind us. It is the French Ambassador, who is coming to visit the Green Mosque, preceded, as Oriental etiquette requires, by a handsome janissary all embroidered with gold.

We had told him of our modest friends the imams, and he walked over to our little contemplation platform, not at all surprised to find us sitting there. The imams stand at his approach and we make the introductions: "Our friends, the imams of the Green Mosque!" "Our Ambassador!"

Then the Ambassador, with his charming manners, would like to shake their hands. And the imams take his hand quite simply, neither obsequious nor embarrassed; like all Orientals, they, too, have their distinction and grandeur. Besides, in this country where great and small are used to sitting down together to talk, dream, and drink the same inoffensive things in the shade, the powerful do not frighten the humble away.

And, when the time comes for the man who is nearly a century old

The interior of the Ulu Mosque.

Turkish confectionery in Bursa.

to go down the stairs again with a trembling step, the Ambassador motions to the gilded janissary to help him, and he does so with obvious respect.

Now we must leave the Green Mosque, this delightful, unique spot, and perhaps forever: we are returning to Europe tomorrow.

Our last look at the funerary kiosk of Sultan Mehmet I is unforgettable. Through the stained glass window that seems made of jewels, the sun, very low now, throws clusters of colored rays on the pink and silver catafalque, and the great funereal object thus stands out, shining in the blue half-light of these depths covered with precious green faience.

We go through Bursa for the last time; it is already invaded by the darkness of the evening. Twilight has begun under the plane trees and the bushy arches of the vine arbors in the little streets where the whole population is now seated after the peaceful labors of the day, smoking sleep-inducing hookahs-common people in short vests of red or blue with a cashmere sash around their waist; on their noble heads, a black-tasseled tarboosh surrounded by a slender silk turban; well-educated people, rich people in long robes, with bulky turbans in white or green muslin; all chatting together, awaiting the signal for the maghrib.[23] They will all pray together. The heat has gone with the light, and everywhere one hears the cool noise of the fountains.

Before returning to our lodgings, we would like to see hedge-cut funerary landscape around the Muradiye mosque once again.

The day has already turned into twilight and the bats are awakening when we enter this enclosure. We walk through the tall grass, almost reverential in the half-night of the giant plane trees; their branches seem like torsos or trunks of monsters, and everywhere rosebushes surround them-garlands of red roses or garlands of pink roses. We meet no one, and the stone kiosks of the dead sultans all seem closed off, lugubrious now in this darkness.

We are leaving. But now, from the depths of the green darkness, the Imam who had welcomed us yesterday suddenly appears. He walks toward us smiling, like one who is already our friend:

"Oh! Why have you come so late?" Indeed, everything is closed.
In his belt he is carrying the big keys to the tombs and he offers to open them for us. We ask him to show us only Prince Mustafa's tomb, because of the marvelous faience tiles inside it.

But it is too dark inside under the double cover of the cupola and the trees: we can no longer make out the lapis blues or the coral reds of the enameled flowers; the magnificent wall surface seems no more than a tapestry with sad, outdated designs, in monotonous grays; the catafalque is disturbing, with its human head-gear; there seems to be a vague corpse-like smell in the air.

Yes, let us go. Behind us, the old gate creaks as it closes again; we follow the paths out, under the thickened dome of the leaves, between the garlands of roses, on that wild grass special to cemeteries.

And as we would like to gather some of those roses-"Just wait!" says the Imam. He disappears behind the branches, but soon returns carrying others, absolutely fragrant, roses used to make exquisite Oriental perfume.

The closed night, the moonless night sparkling with stars, finds me at my window, still looking out at the country I'm going to leave tomorrow morning, the plain below, magnificently green in the daylight and intensely black now.

Then I recall that ugly little plume of smoke in such a hurry to run through the woods, which the nearly hundred-year-old Imam had pointed out to me with a gesture from the top of his delightful terrace; and I think I can still hear that *Yetişir! Yetişir!* ("That's enough! that's enough!") repeated

[23] Evening prayer; one of the five obligatory daily times of prayer.

Pierre Loti (at the left) sitting in front of a café in Bursa.

two or three times, in the way of the old men of the East who like to emphasize their thoughts by repetitions.

Oh, yes! That is indeed enough, in fact too much, unfortunately! That is how the unhappy agitation of the Occident is going to swoop down on the old capital of the Osmanlis; and it is how everything will disappear, quickly, quickly, like a stream that nothing can stop: everything-peace, dreams, prayer and faith.

Jenny Fensom
1st February
2007

JENNY FENSOM

CAT ETUDES

An Anthology of
Rescued and Companion Cats

<><><><><>

Edited and Published
d'Arblays Press

ALSO by Jenny Fensom

WAG TALES (2005)

This Edition first published in 2006 by

d'Arblays Press
23 Brookbank Close
Cheltenham, Gloucestershire

Printed in England by

Creeds the Printers
Broadoak
Bridport, Dorset DT6 5NL

ISBN: 0-954-8646-3-8

A CIP record for this book is available from the British Library.

TO ANTHONY

with thanks
for all your help, encouragement and support

CONTENTS

EDITOR'S PREFACE

If you've ever wondered what a cat, with its ambiguous eyes, is thinking, feeling or planning, then this is the book for you.

Jenny Fensom explores the cat psychology and the feline interaction with humans in such an insightful and delightful way that you cannot fail to enjoy the experience.

The cats in your life will have even more attraction and significance for you after you have read this book, and you will realize that, asleep or awake, your cat has got you in his sights, is watching your every move, and is planning the negotiation of his own. He is certainly not just asleep on the windowsill, as you thought!

How very sad it is, therefore, to remember that not everyone adores the domesticated animal world – be it a feline, a canine, or a working animal – and neither do such creatures always have the necessary care taken of them. So many of them, to the shame of our humanity, have no-one, not a single person, to protect them and take responsibility for their welfare.

Jenny Fensom's book, therefore, heightens our specific awareness of cats and their needs, and it also demonstrates how your own investment in the fascinating lives of cats will, both directly and indirectly, help the whole animal community world wide.

The cat with the half-closed eyes, that you bid goodnight to in his cosy bed, is saying to you "I know that I am so lucky, but do, please, remember us all … "

Margot Collingbourn-Beevers
Editor – d'Arblays Press

2006

FOREWORD

There is nothing quite so reassuring or comforting as sharing your home with a cat. Cats have a peaceful energy, interspersed with a delightful sense of mischief, which makes them perfect and irresistible companions in our everyday lives. Medical evidence shows that those of us who share our lives with cats or dogs are happier and healthier than people who do not - and my own life is certainly more fulfilled through sharing it with my family of 9 cats and 7 dogs, which I have rescued over the years in Asia.

With the purring contentment of a cat on your lap or the boundless joy and energy of a dog letting you know that all's right with the world, I can't help thinking that if we emulated some of their characteristics - taking time to enjoy the wonders of a summer's day, or relaxing by the fire when it's cold - our own lives and lifestyles would be very different and vastly more satisfying than they are today.

Spending time with one of my cats, Elvis, for just one hour would teach most people the best lesson in perseverance that they could ever learn. Named because he "shakes, rattles and rolls" as a result of cerebellum hyperplasia (a neurological disease which affects his balance and coordination), Elvis is a cat who melts your heart with his sheer determination to behave like my other able-bodied cats.

To Elvis it doesn't matter that he can't jump one inch off the ground - if he wants to follow the other cats leaping onto the bed he devises his own inimitable way to do just that. Step by relentless step, he plants each paw into the edge of the mattress, hauling himself higher and higher with all the determination of an Everest ascender, until he successfully reaches the top. Despite setbacks such as a misplaced paw, which send him hurtling earthwards, Elvis never gives up and time after time he sets off on his mission until it is finally accomplished and he is lying, triumphant and happy, on the bed.

Sadly, millions of cats in Asia will never know a warm bed or a loving family, as their lives are filled only with suffering and are all too short. Together with dogs, cats are often viewed as food for the table or fur for the vain, and thousands are brutally slaughtered each day in the hell holes of live animal markets, which heave with the tortured souls of potential companions.

But there is hope from within and if we are to create meaningful, permanent change to this cycle of misery and abuse, we must initiate programmes in Asia which are driven by the community as a whole. Change is already coming from people inside China who see dogs and cats through the same eyes as animal lovers across the world - it is coming from people who have always had an inherent love for animals, but have previously lacked the confidence to speak out. Today, the tide is turning as more and more passionate animal lovers in Asia are finding their voice and joining the call for practices, previously excused as 'culture', to change. They are the voice for the animals today - and Animals Asia is proud to be joining them in sparking and accelerating far-reaching solutions for animals and people alike.

Personally, these programmes and successes mean everything to me - and they are already making a world of difference to the lives of animals that previously had no hope. Elvis and my other best friends have made my world happy and complete - and I couldn't look them in the eyes unless we all tried to do the same for the millions of cats and dogs across Asia that still desperately need our help.

Jill Robinson MBE
Founder & CEO
Animals Asia Foundation

www.animalsasia.org

PRELUDE AND INTRODUCTION

THE TWELVE OFFICE CATS

==================

PRELUDE

The door bell rang and a small boy stood on the threshold with a tiny kitten in his arms. The light from the lamp shone on his glasses and lit up his halo of flaxen hair. It was Michael who lived in the village. 1 October 1980

THE TWELVE OFFICE CATS

Tortoiseshell Polly was the first,
Then starving Ollie always wanting more,
Affable Bag puss, fluffy, black and white,
Mistress Minnie Mouser moves in next door.
Calico Kate with sunburned ears,
William Wordsworth, such a handsome lad,
Then tabby Willoughby named after
Jane Austen's famous cad.
Smoke grey Kizzy's innocent life
Ends with the scream of a firework bang.
Next roly-poly Mimi and
His Imperial Highness Siamese Kang.
Meek little Aubrey finds peace and calm
In his final twilight year,
Now cheeky Chivers rules the roost,
The only kitten to have resided here!

ETUDE I : POLLY 1980 -1994

Polly had to be smuggled in because my mother was not at all keen on cats. She liked dogs, horses and birds, but cats and small animals like guinea pigs, hamsters, mice and rats met with her severe disapproval.

I remember her saying once that when she was a young child, living at home with her parents, five sisters and a brother, they had kept a cat mainly for catching the mice in the house. Mum and her siblings were playing cards round the table one day and suddenly the family puss made a dart at Mum and bit her on the leg for no reason. Why she was singled out for attack from the other children was a mystery. Probably this solitary incident coloured and influenced her opinion of cats for ever after. I know she frequently referred to it in later years with great indignation.

But in the last few years of her life, even she would be the first to admit that she "Quite liked old Poll"!

This was surely due to the sweetness of Polly's character. She was dark tortoiseshell in colour, very slender with long graceful legs. She had a way of stretching out her paw to you, head on one side, and giving you a gentle pat; I never ever remember her showing her claws.

She had been abandoned with her kittens and taken into the local veterinary surgery: poor Polly and her little ones were in a very sorry state. Homes were found easily for the kittens when they were well enough, but no one wanted Polly. My friend Sue, who was head nurse at the vets, told me about her and I went to see her on the quiet without mentioning it to Mum.

As soon as I saw her I knew I had to have her. Sue sang her praises and said she was the nicest-natured cat you could ever wish to meet! So home she came with me, and my mother was led to believe that the long-legged tortoiseshell cat that kept appearing in the garden and looking down at her in the kitchen from the brick pillar outside, with a quizzical expression on her triangular face, was in fact a stray cat or one that lived nearby and fancied our garden.

"Don't you dare feed her!" she would say. "She'll only keep coming back and we'll never be rid of her!"

So the weeks went by and gradually Mum accepted her as one of the family. She was never allowed into the house because we had Tom, our wire fox terrier at the time, and there would have been ructions between the two. Tom was still a puppy and a typical terrier. I dared not push my luck too far, so Polly slept in the workroom adjoining the house where I used to clip and groom dogs. She never minded the dogs, was quite unfazed by them, and indeed she behaved a bit like a dog herself.

She would follow me across the fields on walks with Tom and old Bosun, the one-eyed terrier cross, who I had found as a stray just before I took Polly home. He was indifferent to Polly and they would sleep together in the same basket - Polly snuggled up on his blind side - until he realized that she was there and then he would get out and leave her, not wishing to be seen to be sharing his bed with a cat!

She was very popular with some of the neighbours, often visiting the older people nearby when she wanted a change of company. She also proved to be a great catcher of mice and was once seen with a young rat in her mouth. This was probably a legacy from the days when she had to fend for herself and feed her young family.

To the day she died, Mum never knew the truth about Polly's origins; she may have suspected something, but she never said. I am glad, though, that she had known and grown fond of at least one cat in her lifetime, even though it took seventy-odd years for it to happen! So we had Polly for about 14 years. She was always healthy and strong, never needing much veterinary attention.

The highlight of her life was when she won a lovely red rosette for 'Character Cat of the Show' in a local charity cat show, back in the town of Dunstable where she had first been found wandering. I was very proud of her as I was not expecting her to win anything with all the competition from the other exotic breeds and beautifully-groomed show cats present. However, obviously the judges liked her placid nature and affectionate disposition and she was given the award.

The only time she acted out of character was when we were having an extension built on the back of the house and she disappeared for about 6 weeks. We knew she was around as she had been sighted in the neighbourhood. She just would not come near the house. The weather was turning colder, it must have been autumn, so one day I decided to make a determined effort to find her and bring her home. I had the sudden idea of going out just before dusk to the large, overgrown garden at the end of our road, where all the cats used to congregate, and calling her.

I went along the road and entered the old lady's garden where I suspected she was and softly called her name. Almost immediately, to my relief, I heard a low, huffy growling noise in the distance. I knew at once it was Polly and eventually there was a rustling in the undergrowth and there she was, moving low down on her stomach, edging suspiciously towards me.

I was very pleased to have her back safe; my brother and I had missed and worried about her. It was obviously the disruption to her life style and routine that had upset her and she had gone off. She was not going to return on her own, oh no, we had to go to find and find her! She was still a bit miffed for a few days on her return but eventually accepted the changes and didn't ever stray again.

She lived for about 15 years with us and then the signs of old age and infirmity began to show. She lost a lot of weight, her appetite went, and clearly she was no longer enjoying life. The vet suggested an operation that might save her and against my better judgement I agreed. I regretted having put her through the ordeal: she passed away on the operating table.

"Lovely natured cat," the young vet nurse said to me "she was purring away right up to the end." I can believe that, I thought sadly, as I collected her from the surgery to be brought back for burial in her beloved garden. Even Mum had a soft spot for old Poll.

POLLY

ETUDE II : OLIVER 1982 – 1995

My brother Anthony was responsible for the next feline to share our lives. It was during the hot summer of 1982 when Oliver, or Ollie, first made his appearance. It had been very hot that summer and my brother had noticed this very thin black cat hovering timidly on our front drive. He put out some water for him and casually remarked to Mum and me that there was a strange cat in the vicinity.

Polly was not very happy about the intruder and kept seeing him off whenever he came near. However, the poor little chap persisted and eventually we put down some dishes of cat food for him, at the spot where he used to come at the same time each evening. He would devour his food hungrily, keeping a wary eye out for Polly.

At first he wouldn't let us get near him. He was a plain little scrap with bandy front legs, and in each one of his ears was a v-shaped notch.

Eventually he came to trust us, and as the weather became colder and wetter he plucked up the courage and settled in with Polly in my workroom. He was the very opposite of her. Polly was always relaxed and at ease with herself, her surroundings and everyone she encountered. Poor Ollie on the other hand was tense, on edge, ready to fly off in a panic at the smallest sound or anything that occurred to startle him. His claws were always unsheathed; he kept tensing and releasing them all the while, fidgeting from one paw to the other as he looked up at you. His main concern was food, getting it, eating it and then always on the outlook for more. Hence he became known as Oliver, always asking for more!

We concluded that he had belonged to a local family who had left him behind when they left the neighbourhood. There had been four children and I think he had been teased and mistreated, which accounted for his wary, nervous disposition. I was to receive many an undeserved scratch or a nip in the thirteen or so years we had him. He was not that old when he first appeared, probably only two, but he had the look of age about him even then. As it is often remarked of the human race that he or she had an old head on young shoulders, so it was with poor Ollie. His early years had been traumatic, a struggle for existence, and the anxious, world-weary look remained with him for the rest of his life.

He and Polly ignored one another most of the time. She accepted him with a calm philosophy. She knew she had first place in the hierarchy.

Ollie never strayed far out of the garden. He was content to stay where he knew the food was in good supply, whereas Polly was much more adventurous and confident and roamed all over the village and surrounding fields. We would often find him hiding in an old cardboard box under a bench, or sometimes sitting upright in a box on its end, so that he looked like a solemn sentry on duty.

His favourite place in summer was in the middle of the compost heap. Anthony came across him one hot summer afternoon and was surprised at how hot he felt underneath. He remarked that it was a wonder he hadn't caught fire!

In spite of his homely, unassuming appearance Oliver attracted quite a lot of attention from various people. When we had the extension built on the back of the house he stayed where he felt safest, unlike Polly who took off in a huff. The builders always asked after him and made a fuss of him, and a young girl who helped me with the cattery became especially fond of him. He sometimes ventured into the churchyard that adjoined our garden during the warmer weather, but again always sitting in the hedge, never in full view. He was a strange little creature, always in the background, content to watch the world go by.

When he was put to sleep following kidney failure, at the estimated age of thirteen, it was surprising how many of my customers missed him and asked after him.

I was glad that he chose our house to live in, after being so heartlessly deserted; he might have turned feral after a time and spent the rest of his days living rough and killing mice and birds, or scrounging out of bins. If I had taken him to the local sanctuary I doubt if anyone would have taken him, due to his ordinary appearance. Black cats often go overlooked in such places.

Unlike my mother, my father loved cats and had owned a black one when he was a boy. Then he developed asthma and sadly the cat had had to go.

Dad died not long before Polly and Oliver came to live with us. I wondered who was responsible for pointing them in the right direction!

OLIVER

ETUDE III : BAG PUSS 1987 - 1995

Gladstone Bags was one of those cats
With a white shirt front and matching spats.
He was the most epicurean cat of all cats
He died of a diet of lambs liver and sprats.

I can never understand the mentality of people who take on an eight-week-old kitten or puppy, keep it for seven or eight years, and then abandon it at the veterinary surgery because they no longer want to pay for the annual injections.

This was what had happened to our third cat to join the family, a large fluffy black and white neutered tom, originally called Zippy.

In the eighties and nineties I helped a local animal charity to find homes for unwanted dogs, cats, and other small domestic pets. I soon became known to the veterinary nurses in the local practices, and would frequently get calls from them when they had boarded a cat, dog, or rabbit for some time, and the vet in charge of the practice was putting pressure on the soft-hearted staff, to move or re-home the animal, or otherwise dispose of it.

Thus it was that after receiving a call from a concerned nurse, I became the owner of eight-year-old Zippy. He had been at the practice for several weeks because his heartless owners had brought him for his annual booster - and then refused to pay the increased price. He proved to be the most affable and laid-back cat of all the twelve I have owned over the last twenty-odd years.

I changed his name from Zippy to Gladstone Bags, and eventually shortened it to Bag puss. Zippy did not suit him at all: he may have zipped about like lightning as a kitten, but in all the years I owned him, I never saw him move much beyond a leisurely amble! He would lay out in the sunshine, watching the birds a few yards away, without so much as a whisker-twitch of interest.

He had the most affectionate disposition and never once showed his claws. I took him to a junior school in Dunstable one afternoon to be introduced to a mixed class of lively eight-year-olds. It was all part of pet awareness week which my friend Toni, an ex school teacher, had helped to organize. Between us we took several small pets, including Sophie my tortoise, Toni's collie Fennel, and Bag puss.

The local press were there and photographed Bags with the children. In spite of being mauled around and bundled from one pair of eager little hands to another, he retained his good humour, and posed importantly for the photographer. I thought in fact that he looked like a benevolent Mr-Chips-type character, surrounded by his adoring pupils. All that was missing was his mortar board.

He kept to his own territory in the garden, ignoring Polly and Oliver if he encountered them. They were quite happy to keep to their areas and there was rarely any fighting between them. This was the advantage of a large garden.

As the years passed, he started to visit a nearby bungalow where an elderly man lived who used to feed all the cats in the neighbourhood. The inevitable happened and he encouraged Bags into his bungalow with luxury food such as liver, fried sprats and fresh milk. I was only too happy for Bags to visit the man and his wife and keep them company. Cats, unlike dogs, can sometimes be fickle at heart and take up residence where and with whom they choose.

So Bags spent most of his daylight hours with the old couple who fed him on food every day which, in my opinion, was much too rich for him. Liver in small portions is all right perhaps, once a fortnight, as a special treat, but Bags was getting large amounts every day, plus cows' milk - which I never give to the cats.

I approached the old man one day and asked him if he and his wife would like to keep Bags for themselves. "Oh, no. We don't want to encourage him, we don't want to have him in at night. We couldn't afford the vet's fees - we are only on a pension."

BAG PUSS

So the inevitable happened. Bags would come home at night and every following morning the end product of his rich diet would be left in the office, in the bath I used for the dogs. It went on day after day until, at last, I knew I had to confront the man and request him either to take on Bags permanently or to stop giving him such rich food.

It was like banging my head against a brick wall. The man didn't listen to a word of what I said. He kept insisting the cat was hungry and kept coming for food. I couldn't get through to him that it was only cupboard love. Of course, he wasn't going to eat tinned and dry food from me, however good the quality, when there was luxury food on offer only a short distance away.

Harsh words were exchanged. I flared up and told the man he was doing it on purpose to make it look as if I was neglecting Bags. This at last made an impact, and with an unpleasant look and a wag of a finger he said one day I would be sorry for what I had said to him and he went into his bungalow and banged the door.

This was not an easy time for me. I was just recovering from the shock of a broken hip, and was not feeling like having to deal with issues such as this. The man's threat lurked in the back of my mind, and was to take on undue significance with what was to happen in the future.

I think Bags would have lived longer if during his later years he had not been fed on such rich food. As it was, he succumbed to liver cancer and I had to have him put to sleep. He went very thin and was sick all the time. His last days were not happy ones and I resolved not to let him be operated on, as it would not have extended his life for very much longer.

My memories of him were happy. I could not blame him for seeking others for companionship. All cats prefer a one-to-one relationship, and he did have to share my affections with so many more pets.

However it was clear that the old couple would have gone on killing him with kindness until he died without veterinary attention. At least I spared him that fate, and he had the dignified end all loved pets deserve. He lived with us for seven years and was about 15 when we lost him.

ETUDE IV : KATY 1988 - 1990

I only have very hazy memories of poor little calico Kate, with her sunburned ears.

Perhaps it was because she was only with us for two to three years. The one photograph I have of her is with me holding her. She was rather a peevish little thing and disliked being handled or touched, but then with those poor ears who could blame her?

She arrived just before one Christmas about 15 years ago, via my friend Toni who was very much involved with pet rescue. Toni and her partner Ray lived in a small Victorian terraced cottage which was full of abandoned pets of all kinds.

There were at least twelve cats living indoors; three dogs, Poppy, Fennel and Cayenne; a resident tortoise; and a selection of rabbits and guinea pigs who inhabited the garden.

The cats were all named after herbs and spices. I can only remember a few of them now: a large fluffy ginger tom named Nutmeg; Parsley, a petite little tabby-and-white female; Coriander and Thyme; Toni's special favourite, Rush puss, a long-haired fluffy tabby; and several others whose names I have forgotten.

The little cottage had a cellar, and down there lived two anti-social cats who were not allowed to mix with the others. They inhabited a kind of shady criminal feline underworld. The Codfathers of Bedfordshire Feline Lowlife in fact! One of them, Peppercorn, Toni had nicknamed Millwall. The evil deeds of T S Elliot's Growltiger had nothing on the crimes committed by Millwall!

Toni had a very dry, ironic humour, and when I was introduced to Millwall I could make the connection. I was warned to descend the cellar steps carefully in case my ankles were seized! Had he been human, rather than feline, he would have been the equivalent of one of the more thuggish type of Millwall football fan. When I first encountered him there he was, sitting on his haunches, boxing away with his paws and aiming punches at the air, while at the same time swearing away vociferously at his fellow cell companion, whose name I can't recall. Millwall was a fluffy, scruffy, black cat with a small amount of white on his chest. His eyes were crossed and he squinted malevolently at you if you dared even look at him. He really needed a leather punch ball to occupy him.

Yes, he certainly had attitude - or perhaps even cattitude?

Toni was not amused when I suggested this to her. Only a devoted cat lover like Toni would have given him house-room. "Poor Millwall," she would say indulgently, "he can't help his anti-social ways. He would have ended up feral if we hadn't taken pity on him". He and his companion lived a contented enough life, with plenty of good food and the pursuit of mice in the cellar. Many cats have lived in conditions a lot worse.

So one evening, just before Christmas, I received a call from Toni saying that Win, the lady who ran the local rescue charity, had taken in a small, elderly calico cat that had been found living rough on an allotment in the town. Someone had taken pity on the poor thing and had taken it to the shelter.

But it was Christmas and there was no more room at the inn.

Toni rang me in desperation: "How many cats have you got, Jenny?" she pleaded.

"Three", I replied, warily, "and that's enough".

"Jenny, if you've got three, you might as well even the score and have four!" Toni pleaded, eloquently. "Please, it is Christmas and, poor little scrap, she's never had much."

So this clinched it and come the next day Katy had a roof over her head, a comfortable warm bed, and a roast turkey Christmas dinner!

Her last remaining years were happy although she went missing for one week and was eventually found in a garage at the old rectory in the village. She had wandered off there one summer evening from the churchyard, which was the favourite haunt of all our cats, become disorientated, and had somehow got shut in.

I spent a worried week looking for her and then the lady at the rectory phoned me and described her and I went and fetched her. She was very thin and stressed, so I saw to it that she didn't get the chance to wander again.

She had to have both the tips of her ears amputated eventually: they had become cancerous and it was the only option. This was the start of her decline, and not long afterwards her kidneys failed, so we decided it was kindest to have her put to sleep.

We buried her in her favourite spot in front of the cattery where she used to sleep among the marigolds. Part of her colouring matched the vibrant orange of the blooms themselves and it was sometimes difficult to distinguish her there in the flower bed. Rest in peace little Katy cat, you deserve to.

I always associate Katy with Toni, who helped me through a very worrying time when I was having such aggression from a new neighbour, who had moved in on our boundary. He had started a campaign against my boarding kennels and eventually, to keep the peace, I closed them down.

KATY with JENNY

It was Toni who boosted my morale during that difficult time and encouraged me to change to a cattery. She sent many rescued cats to me that she had re-homed, and so started me off on a different pathway. Her mischievous sense of fun helped me through many a gloomy moment. I only had to phone her or call in at her little cottage and she would find something funny in the situation, to cheer me up and put things into perspective.

She has moved from the area now and I do miss her. Still deeply involved in animal rescue and fund-raising, she and Ray deserve special mention in Cat Etudes.

ETUDE V : MINNIE 1989 - 1991

All day she sits upon the stair or on the steps or on the mat:
She sits and sits and sits and sits - and that's what makes a Gumbie cat!

Old Possum's Book of Practical Cats   T S Eliot

Mistress Minnie Mouser made it clear from the start that she was only passing through! Whereas before Polly, Oliver, Bag puss, and Katy were only too pleased to find a comfortable home, Minnie's attitude was altogether different!

I brought her home from the cat refuge centre, where she had been caged for far longer than was good for her.

She had a very pretty face, with a placid expression, a tabby-tortoiseshell combination with a faint gold stripe. I was surprised no-one had offered her a home since she was so attractive but, as I was later to discover, Mistress Minnie had an anti-social problem: she would not use a litter tray. At first she was just content to sit in the same place all day long, contemplating the space in front of her with unblinking pale green eyes.

A thinking cat!

I rightly deduced that she was mulling things over and deciding to herself that the accommodation was not up to her required standard.

MINNIE

Win, at the shelter, was a bit elusive about Minnie's origins, but it soon became clear that Mistress Minnie Mouser was very much her own puss and was just for the moment biding her time!

Our next-door neighbours had just lost their very ancient tabby cat, Mog, and were not really thinking of obtaining a replacement. However, Minnie had other ideas and it was not too long before she began to pay discreet visits into their garden.

If ever a cat lived up to the feline principle of looking out for its best interests, Minnie did. She was obviously not prepared to share the household with the four other cats and five dogs.

"Oh no, thank you very much, I know on which side of the fence I want to be. I prefer a quiet life away from the rough and tumble existence of this place. The vicar and his wife's home is much more to my liking. Quiet, civilised, and all the attention for me alone. Mind you, don't think I don't appreciate what you've done for me. I could see my troubles were coming to an end when you came to the shelter. Muggins written all over you. Thank you for taking me in. It was better than being cooped up in that cage all day, and you do a nice tin of tuna too. But it's not quite the sort of establishment I had in mind. I knew before I came to the refuge that I had nowhere to go and had to forage for food and live under a hedgerow, but now I have found somewhere which measures up to what I deserve. So goodbye and thanks again; perhaps when this new couple go away on holiday you can come round and visit and feed me. I still want to keep in touch, but I'll stay here though, if you don't mind, the whole house to myself and, if they come up to scratch and satisfy my requirements, I might catch the odd mouse for them and, who knows, I might start to use a litter tray."

ETUDE VI : KIZZY 1991 - 1996

I knew it would not be easy for me to tell Kizzy's story, but I could not write Cat Etudes and leave her out.

She came from the same vet's surgery as Bag puss had done, four years earlier. It was the same nurse who contacted me and the same reason for her need to be re-homed: a refusal by her previous owner to pay vet bills.

She had a skin allergy which was responding well to treatment, but it meant she would always have to have medication. She was only about three years old, an unusual smokey-blue colour, with a faint gold stripe. Not the prettiest of cats, with a flat face; some pedigree in her looks, maybe British Blue, which accounted for her very placid disposition.

She settled into a corner of my storeroom, unlike Minnie, making it clear that this is where she intended to make her home. I only kept her in for a few days because I could see she had a contented nature and would not wander far. Nor did she ever do so, except once, in the five years we were lucky enough to have her.

She darted like quicksilver about the garden and adjoining churchyard, climbing trees, stalking birds but not bothering to kill any. A happy little soul, the youngest cat we had owned since Polly and Oliver's earliest years. They were now quite old and beginning to ail; Katy had gone; Minnie was settled happily next door, and we still had Bag puss, although he was often in the old couple's bungalow.

Kizzy behaved more like a dog than a cat, and would often follow me on walks, as Polly used to in her young days. I remember one particular late spring evening when I called on my friend Nikki who lived in the village, and I took the short cut to her house through the churchyard, with Kizzy loping along behind me. I must have stayed there chatting for about two hours and it was dark when I came out. Kizzy had been waiting underneath Nikki's car in the drive all that time. She came out and rubbed herself round my legs and then started off up the drive to cross over the road, to go back through the churchyard.

I hesitated before following her, feeling rather foolish. It was now dark and the cemetery could be a bit spooky, but it was a longer walk round by the road, and Kizzy was waiting patiently for me on the other side.

I set off after her and she flitted along in front of me with her tail carried high in the air: it was as if she was saying "Come along, if a little creature like me isn't afraid of the dark and the graves you shouldn't be either!"

Dear little Kizzy. Whenever I think of her I remember my late father's words not long before he died: "Jenny will always be all right if she has plenty of dogs and cats to look after". But he should have rephrased it: "Jenny will always be all right with plenty of dogs and cats to look after her!" He got it wrong.

So she lived with us for five years; her coat improved and grew thick and glossy with the healthy outdoor life. She did not need any medication, her allergy disappeared and there were seldom visits to the vet, apart from her yearly boosters.

At the time of her untimely end we just had the three cats, Kizzy, Wordsworth, and Willoughby, who feature in the next two chapters. Polly, Oliver, and Bag puss had all gone, each aged 15: a good long life-span for a cat.

We now had two other male cats living with Kizzy: the self important Wordsworth, and the aloof Willoughby. The three bonded together well and life was happy and carefree.

Until one hot July evening, when there was a jazz concert and firework display at the old rectory in the village. There was also a stray dog running free that weekend and no-one could get near to catch it.

I had decided to shut Kizzy into a cat pen that evening because of the fireworks but, because she hated it so much, I changed my mind and released her. She darted off along the path leading to the churchyard and that was the last time I ever saw her. She had never gone off before, not even for half a day. When she did not appear the next morning for breakfast, I had the gut feeling that something bad had happened to her.

In the miserable days that followed my brother, who was as upset as I was, searched the village and put up cards in shop windows. We contacted the vet surgeries and left her details. No one responded: she had vanished into thin air.

Nagging away in the back of my mind were the words of the old man who used to feed Bag puss: "You will be sorry one day". His threat took on new significance, and my mind went into overdrive. I thought he had taken Kizzy and given her away to someone out of the area. I would never find her, never see her again.

Some of the neighbours were more sympathetic than others. A lot shrugged it off as of no consequence, after all we had two other cats, and the dogs had always meant more to me than the cats. I think they thought I was doing a prima donna act, in order to draw attention to myself. It was not the case at all. I loved each pet in a different way and Kizzy was special, so sweet-natured and inoffensive. I dreaded to think what might have happened to her.

During that first nightmare week of her disappearance I went through a living hell. My brother (who had taken time off work) and I called on the old man in the bungalow and asked tactfully if he had seen Kizzy. He appeared concerned and said he had not seen her for a long time. We had to believe him. I think everyone thought I was over-reacting to his previous threat, when I had asked him to stop feeding Bag puss.

The whole sad episode escalated into a full-scale drama. Things I had said were twisted round and repeated out of context. One neighbour made me feel like a criminal, saying I had gone round to the old man in the bungalow accusing him of stealing Kizzy. Life in the surrounding neighbourhood changed for me for ever, it was never the same again.

After about three weeks, on one Saturday afternoon, Anthony my brother came in from the front garden looking very serious and sad. "I've found her," he said quietly. "She's in the field opposite, can't think why we didn't look there in the first place."

We went across the road to the field and her poor remains were there. There could be no mistaking her distinctive colouring. We believe she had met her end the very night of the firework display: had taken flight across the road, probably with the stray dog chasing her. We would never know for sure.

Dear little Kizzy did not deserve to die in this way. I blamed myself for not shutting her in that night.

She would not have blamed me, however. Cats love their freedom and she had enjoyed five years of healthy, unrestricted country living. But it took me a long time to come to terms with her loss, and to this day I still feel sad when I think of her.

KIZZY

ETUDE VII : WORDSWORTH 1993/4 – 2000

We called him Wordsworth because he arrived when the daffodils were in bloom.

He was a handsome, distinguished, long-haired tabby and white, with a charismatic aura of mystery about him that was evident from the start. People to whom he was introduced noticed and remarked upon it. He calmly acknowledged their admiring comments, taking it in his leisurely stride as he promenaded his territory and surrounding neighbourhood. Here was a cat that held himself in high regard. Moreover, he was introduced into the household by a family connection, which made him all that more special.

One day I received a concerned phone call from a distant relative of my late mother's family. Bill was the younger, unmarried brother of my Uncle Harold who was married to my mother's older sister Aunt Eva. In the post-war years, when families were larger, there were always lots of often unmarried, adopted aunts and uncles around. Although he was not a blood relative he was always known to me as Uncle Bill. He once came along on a family holiday and I remember him looking after our first black poodle, George, several times when we needed a pet-sitter. He was a great lover of animals and although we lost touch with him over the years I always remembered him with affection.

He stayed single all his life and eventually moved into sheltered accommodation. This was at the time when he was told by a lady in a neighbouring flat about Wordsworth. This cat, obviously either lost or abandoned, had been visiting houses in the neighbourhood. Bill's friend had fed him for some time but, because pets were not allowed in the flats, had not dared to encourage him in

So Bill rang me up and told me about this beautiful cat who must have belonged to someone at some time. There had been no reports of a cat missing that matched his description. Please could I help; the kind lady was getting very stressed over the whole issue.

So I went along to the flats and there lay Wordsworth on the sofa, looking very much at home. I fell for his charms straight away and promised Bill and his friend that I would first of all make more extensive enquiries regarding his former owner. If this proved unsuccessful I would find him a home myself or, if it came to it, I would keep him myself. I had decided this anyway as soon as I had seen him!

I contacted all the vets in the surrounding areas but he was never claimed. I had him neutered and he settled comfortably into the menagerie. His nature was very gentle and very friendly. Neighbours soon got to know him and remarked on his gentlemanly manners. I felt he needed a distinguished name, and with the spring timing of his arrival, William, after Bill, and Wordsworth, after one of my favourite poets, seemed appropriate.

About 18 months after his arrival a surprising coincidence happened. It was the early morning of New Year's Eve, 1995. I was going up the garden, to feed the cats in the cattery, when I fell heavily on the slushy snow which hid a sheet of treacherous black ice underneath. For the first two weeks of 1996 I was in the Luton and Dunstable Hospital with a fractured hip. It was a traumatic time for me and something I would rather forget and put behind me. I found myself in a very vulnerable position, not only physically but psychologically as well.

Several days before I was due to be discharged, there was a new admission to the ward. The lady was in for knee surgery and as we chatted and exchanged names and addresses it transpired that she was the lady who had been feeding Wordsworth, and who had been so worried about him. She was delighted to hear that he was very well and happy and she was very impressed with the name I had chosen for him. She then revealed that she loved poetry and had written a poem about her much-loved Scottish Terrier, McGregor. She gave me a copy of it and I still have it to this day. It was strange that we should both meet up in this way. I'm glad I was able to reassure her that the stray cat she had befriended was living happily in the country, after wandering the streets of a busy area in the town.

Later that year Wordsworth won a trophy in a local cat show for the Best Rescued Male Cat. He took it all calmly and in his stride: I was more excited than he was!

Unfortunately, as Wordsworth grew older his placid good nature seemed to change and he became rather unpredictable if you were stroking or making a fuss of him. He would turn his head suddenly and give you a sharp nip, or strike out with his paw without any reason. I noticed this happened after he had been enticed into a neighbour's conservatory. They were not genuine cat lovers and had always made a mockery of my love for animals. I was aware of the nature of the two men of the house and I believe Wordsworth had been teased by them and that it had altered his entire nature.

I felt sad about this and wondered why people could behave in such a manner. These people knew how much pleasure my pets gave to me but they just couldn't leave the cat alone.

This did not alter my affection for Wordsworth since I knew the reason for this sudden change of character. He was not to blame, any more than Bag puss was for being fed on unsuitable food by another annoying neighbour.

WORDSWORTH

I think he was about 4 when he came to live with us. We had him for perhaps eight years and then he developed the usual ailments of old age and was finally put to sleep when nothing more could be done for him.

The most photogenic and handsome of all our cats, he regained more of his original affectionate disposition towards the end, when he came to rely on us for care and attention.

Bill passed away only a short while ago. I am glad he called on me to help all those years ago. Wordsworth gave me a lot of pleasure in the time he spent with me. I will never forget, either, Mrs Walker, the lady who looked after him and whom I think I could regard as a kindred spirit.

ETUDE VIII : WILLOUGHBY 1995 – 2004

He was just a tabby cat
Of the ordinary kind
When his owner died in a rented flat
Poor Willy got left behind.

Everything had to go
Including the old man's cat
The landlord didn't want to know
The tenant was dead
And that was that!

So I brought him home with me
I found him sitting in an old armchair.
The look on his face spoke volumes
"My master's gone, but where?"

I'd already got two cats
And did not want a third,
Kizzy and Wordsworth were good mates,
They sat together and conferred!

They treated him with suspicion
As cats are wont to do
He backed off in submission
He'd show them later who was who!

He'd never seen a garden
Or been near a pond.
On his first day out he fell in
I fished him out, forged a bond.

Now it's tuna, salmon, trout on the menu
"Is there anything else sir, you require?"
Willie the street-wise alley cat
Is now Sir Willoughby country squire!

When the next cat came along I had only two others, Wordsworth and Kizzy. All the rest, Polly, Oliver, Katie and Bag puss, had, over a period of fifteen years, departed to the happy hunting grounds. However, Mistress Minnie Mouser was still alive and being lovingly cosseted next door.

It was the smallest amount of felines present since the early days of Polly and Oliver. Two was enough everyone said and I tended to agree. Wordsworth and Kizzy had formed a bond and I would sometimes catch them unawares, playing like kittens together.

So when a lady, who used to board her dog with me, rang and said that there was a large tabby cat left abandoned in a rented flat after his owner had died, I was at first reluctant to become involved.

However, the lady was very concerned, and after a bit more persuasion I agreed to go to the flat in the middle of Luton town centre and collect him. It would only be temporary, I said firmly, until he could be re-homed somewhere else.

The landlord let me into the little flat and there, sitting forlornly on an old armchair, sat a very ordinary-looking middle-aged tabby.

"Whatever is it all about?" he seemed to be thinking as he sat there, "Why has my owner gone away and left me?"

My heart went out to the poor chap. I put him into a carrying cage and took him home. I was undecided what to do with him at first. Wordsworth and Kizzy were such good companions and I did not want to upset the status quo. I thought someone might take him although older cats are always difficult to relocate. Also the dear soul was so ordinary looking, like my dear old Oliver; he would not be able to sell himself very well to prospective owners.

Polly was not a pretty cat but she had had a whimsical charm about her and of course Wordsworth's charismatic appeal got him everywhere. Minnie had a sweet expression, and fluffy cats like Bag puss are always popular choices.

Will had already lashed out a few times when things had not gone to his liking, revealing a waspish little streak in his make-up. He's only got to do that once to a new owner, I thought, and he'll soon be brought back, with his tail between his legs!

He had always lived in the town and there had been no garden or grass in sight at the flat. When I first let him out, he wandered about, puzzled by being, for the first time ever, in a garden with trees, plants and birds singing overhead.

He did not see the small pond in the corner by the fence and suddenly, while momentarily my back was turned, I heard a loud splash and an outraged yowl as he overbalanced and fell straight in!

I fished him out and dried him off, while he suspiciously surveyed his new surroundings. "What sort of a place is this?" he was probably thinking. "And now she's gone and half drowned me. Still, I'll bide my time, beggars can't be choosers and there does seem to be plenty of food around. Pity about those other two cats but I'll soon show them who's boss around here".

Wordsworth and Kizzy accepted him: they were not aggressive cats. In fact, if there was any aggression it was from Will's corner, not theirs.

I decided to name him Willoughby after the raffish cad in the popular film "Sense and Sensibility" which was showing in cinemas at this time. Rather an upmarket sort of name for such a mundane-looking cat, but I thought it might boost his morale a little.

As time passed he settled into his new home, mellowed and became more trusting. He spent most of the daytime asleep in the office, but at night I know he liked to go out on the prowl. He was as good at catching mice as Polly had been and a selection of his trophies would often be found on the office floor. Wordsworth never bothered to catch mice (I think he thought it was beneath him) but Willoughby quickly adapted from town to country life and took his sporting pursuits quite seriously. From streetwise alley cat he became a country squire, stalking importantly round his territory, checking the garden for mice and disposing of them efficiently. In his funny little way I think he may have been showing a little bit of gratitude for being rescued and given a home.

We had him for about nine years. He was a strong old boy and only had to go to the vet once for a dental job. He ate well and became quite selective in his later years, preferring cooked white fish and chicken to ordinary cat food.

It was quite a shock when one Sunday morning I went to open the office door and heard him moaning feebly on the threshold inside. He was lying against the door, very stressed, and both his back legs were paralysed. I carried him over to the desk and, still holding him, dialled the vet's number. Sad at heart, I waited for him to arrive; it was not looking good at all.

The vet diagnosed a pulmonary thrombosis. This had come on quickly and unexpectedly as Will had been his old self the day before.

There was a small chance he might pull through with an injection and medication, but his life would only be prolonged for a few more weeks. I knew Will had had enough as he looked up at me with weary eyes. He was probably older than we had estimated and I knew I would be being selfish to keep him alive when he clearly just wanted to go to sleep and be at peace.

So he slipped quietly away. I was sad for days after, for that cantankerous old fellow had found a place in my heart that would not be easy to replace.

WILLOUGHBY

ETUDE IX : MIMI 1996 –

Just as Wordsworth before her had done, Mimi, our present cat residing in the office, came via a family connection.

My uncle and aunt had lived in the same house in Luton for 53 years. Their late next-door-neighbour, Mary, had moved in at the same time with her husband, Robert. The two young couples had got on well, and in fact it was the ideal neighbour situation, in that they helped each other out in small ways but at the same time respected each other's privacy. On the other side of my uncle and aunt lived Jim and his wife and two daughters, who were also good friends of both Mary and Robert, and my uncle and aunt.

During Mary's later years, Jim always backed her ancient Hillman Minx out of her garage when she wanted to go out.

Mary and Robert had no children and eventually over a period of time Robert became an invalid and died after a long illness. Poor Mary was left a widow, but she had a lot of good friends to help her. She was a lovely person, a tiny bit eccentric and I always thought she had an "other-worldly" aura about her. It was said she often visited the local spiritualist church, probably trying to contact her beloved Robert, her mother, and her aunt, who had all passed away at about the same time. Often such vulnerable ladies become victim to unscrupulous individuals who take mean advantage of people like her.

So Mary went a long way back. I remember her smiling at me over the dividing fence in my uncle's garden and handing me over small nosegays of flowers. She always owned cats, often two together, and I would sometimes go round to her house and play with them.

At the time when I lost Kizzy, Mary, now an elderly lady, was very upset for me and kept asking my uncle and aunt if she had been found. When the worst was known, she sent me a sympathetic message.

Several months after this Mary became very ill and had to be cared for at home. I had heard that up to and during her illness she had been feeding a stray black cat with three kittens.

One morning my aunt phoned me with the sad news that her good friend and neighbour of nearly fifty years had passed away at home. I felt a loss. Mary represented a bygone era of decent, ordinary folk, content with what they had, and happy to help out anyone when they could, with no conditions attached. My uncle and aunt had lost a neighbour in a million.

Several days after Mary's funeral service, which had been held at her own home, I had a mysterious phone call from Jim, the other neighbour, asking if he could come and see me.

He sounded most conspiratorial on the phone.

I might have guessed!

Mary had asked Jim, just before she died, to take the stray black cat to me and find her a home with the three kittens. How could I refuse?

MIMI

Mary had always been a little superstitious and maybe she thought a black cat would bring me some luck, after having first broken my hip and then the tragic death of Kizzy.

So Jim brought the cat over in a zipped-up shopping bag, together with three fluffy black and white kittens in a basket. He handed them over, together with an envelope containing some money that Mary had given him before she died. This was to cover the costs of getting the mother cat spayed. He departed quickly, after enjoining me to promise not to let my aunt and uncle know anything about the transaction! All very cloak and dagger, and to this day I have never discovered the reason for so much secrecy.

The kittens were easy to find homes for. Laura, a young girl who was doing work experience in my cattery, took one of them, and the other two went to a young family living nearby. However, nobody offered to have the mum, whom I had named Mimi.

She was a sweet little cat, jet black all over. I thought about Kizzy, and of course it was not long before Mimi wasn't going anywhere, and she settled in with Wordsworth and Willoughby.

She had been very slender and dainty when she first arrived but after her operation she very quickly started to billow out. I tried to diet her, but it didn't seem to work. She was by no means a greedy cat, she ate very little; it must have been due to hormone changes.

She did not move far from the office, content to sleep most of the time, just emerging into the garden for toilet purposes and then rolling back in again to settle down in her comfortable basket. I think she took the attitude that she had achieved motherhood, brought three kittens into the world and that was it; she'd earned herself a comfortable retirement package. Just bring on the food, make a fuss of me and see that I'm in the warmth of a good home for the rest of my days and, thanks very much, I'll wash my paws of it all!

She is still the same 10 years later. My regular customers make a fuss of her and all exclaim every time they visit the office about her size. New customers ask me if she is pregnant!

The ultimate irony came when I took her for her booster jab and an earnest, keen young vet, new to the practice, rebuked me for allowing her to get so large, remarking that she had a poor quality of life.

I thought of all the pets I had taken in over the years, and here was some officious whippersnapper, young enough to be my daughter, telling me how to care for animals! I counted to ten, paid the bill and swept out of the surgery.

ETUDE X : KANG 1998 – 2004

I used to have Kang to board in my cattery but in those days he was known as Danny, which I didn't think suited him at all.

The lady who owned him at that time told me that she was his third owner. The woman who had bred him had allowed him to run the streets as a very young kitten, and then she had sold him to a couple with young children, who had teased and tormented him.

So his present owner took him on when he was about two and kept him for five years. He was safe with her, she said firmly; oh no, she would never part with Danny. She had another female Siamese and she used to board both of them with me twice a year.

One day I received a distressed phone call. Please could I give Danny a home: he had become jealous of the other cat and was spraying everywhere indoors. They would be soon moving into a new home and her husband was adamant that Danny must go. I replied sympathetically that I was very sorry but I didn't particularly want him spraying in my office either.

Oh, but Danny loved being out of doors, he'd love your garden with all the grass and trees to climb. An old shed would do for shelter!

I tried to persuade her to give him another chance, or to phone Siamese Rescue, but that was no good: Siamese Rescue was full to the brim with cats like Danny, with the same anti-social problem, and hubby was really adamant the cat had to go.

So weakly I gave in and agreed to take him, little knowing what I would be letting myself in for. Once again it was the case that I had three cats, so I may as well even the score and have four!

Wordsworth and Willoughby accepted the exotic stranger quite well, to my surprise. It was Mimi who took a thorough dislike to him, and it lasted all the time he lived with us.

For the first few days I kept him penned up, although he didn't seem too stressed with the change of circumstances. I decided to let him out and he strolled around the garden languidly sizing up his new surroundings. Every now and then he would give a lovely deep YOWEL of approval, while looking up at me with his brilliant searchlight sapphire-blue eyes.

He was a beautiful animal - there was no doubting it - but I was still apprehensive, knowing the nature of the typical Siamese. I seriously wondered whether this would work. They are really one-to-one owner cats, possessive and jealous of sharing affections. There were three others here, and he would either have to take his chance on yet another home, which might take ages to find, while he was kept confined and miserable, or accept the freedom of our large garden and churchyard, where he could come and go as he pleased. He chose the second option.

He soon became well known in the neighbourhood. People were surprised to see a pedigree cat roaming free. He was happy to do this. In the summer he slept in a bed in an old rabbit hutch. He was always within earshot. I only had to call his new name, KANG! Within half a minute I would hear the distinctive vocal response and there he would suddenly appear in front of me. You never really saw him coming; like P G Wodehouse's famous character, Jeeves, there would be a shimmering effect and he was next to you! Perhaps I should have named him Jeeves.

He used to sleep in the office in the winter months in a corner chair. He treated Mimi with aloof distain, ignoring her spitting and the angry swipes with her paw. He was very much aware of his aristocratic breeding and it was quite amusing to notice how he would leap gracefully on to the window ledge and look haughtily down his proud Roman nose at the other three underlings!

Wordsworth might have the literary connections and the glamour, Willoughby was the self-appointed country squire, Mimi had the status of resting opera singer with a diet problem, but here was class, here was pedigree, here was His Imperial Highness Chocolate Point Siamese Kang.

If cattery customers came into the office he would display his elegant figure on the rug in front of them, basking in their admiring comments. "Have you ever seen anyone as magnificent as me?" he seemed to be saying.

Cynthia Mayles, whose cat anecdotes appear in a later chapter, was captivated by him and made a beautiful cross-stitch picture of him which hangs in the office.

At first he fed on ordinary tinned and dried food, with the occasional tuna or chicken treat. Then he had a phase of being very selective and nearly drove me to distraction with his diet whims. He had a craze once for turkey roll, which I knew was not good for him, being too high in salt and additives. This was all he craved however and before long he employed a cunning strategy to get his own way. If turkey roll was not on the menu he went out and slaughtered a bird. That was the deal: blackmail, in other words. There would be a pile of feathers in the garden and no-one to be seen. I knew the culprit. Will only hunted at night, Wordsworth was now too old and frail to bother, and Mimi far too idle. Fortunately this craze soon fizzled out and he went back to eating his former cat food and the birds in the garden were able to relax.

He was determined not to let another male cat on to his territory. Will and Wordsworth were of course already established, but then one day a young tabby and white male cat started to visit the garden and linger around the cattery. I made enquiries, but no-one knew who he belonged to. He was very friendly, cheeky and determined. I am sure he had made up his mind where he was going to live. I was tempted, but Kang had other ideas: it was as if he had read my mind!

He stalked the youngster out of the garden, growling threateningly with both ears laid flat against his head. I had never seen him take exception to any other cat in this way before.

For a while I shut Walter, as I had named him, into an old disused kennel and run. My friend Pam had said her friend's young daughter wanted a cat and Walter would make a good pet. Kang still kept a check on him, circling round the enclosure, spitting and lashing out with his paw. It was quite amusing to watch this exhibition of feline jealousy. Kang was certainly not going to tolerate a younger, handsome male on his territory.

Eventually Walter left for his new home with his delighted young owner, who renamed him Alfie. Kang once again reverted to his usual good nature, regaining his celebrity status as most important resident cat. I do believe Alfie's days would have been numbered if the two had ever met up in the garden.

I had Kang for six years and the last few months of his life were very traumatic: stressful both to himself and to us.

He lost a lot of weight, seldom went out and developed gingivitis. The poor little cat really suffered from those sore gums, which was the prelude to kidney disease. I made endless trips to the vets for various forms of treatment, steroids mostly, and antibiotics for his mouth. He'd improve for a few weeks and then start to go downhill again.

Then he began spraying in the office and I knew then it was time to call it a day and give him a dignified end. I held him while the vet gave him the final injection and he slipped quietly away. My mystical little mandarin man, I used to call him. He always answered in his own inimitable voice when I called him and would appear, as if by magic, in front of me from out of thin air.

I miss him still and would love to own another, but they are not easy cats and at present I must make do with the memory of aristocratic Chocolate Point Siamese Kang.

KANG

ETUDE XI : AUBREY 2002 – 2003

Little Aubrey stayed with us for even less time than Katy all those years ago. Just about one year in fact. If it had not been for another person's meddling and interference, he could have stayed for a lot longer.

Most of the people I meet and work with when rescuing pets, are very dedicated and easy to get along with. We work well together as a team, our main concern and priority being the animal in need of help.

However, over the years there has been one person with whom I have had dealings who always seems to know what's best for whatever dog, cat, etc, there is that's in trouble. Only she knows the best way of handling the situation and everyone else's ideas are rubbished with contempt. Once she kindly informed me that if there were ninety-nine right ways to do anything and only one wrong way I would always choose the latter.

This woman has done her best to lower my confidence on more than one occasion. However, in the case of little Aubrey she made a complete and utter fiasco out of the whole situation, washed her hands of it all, and then left me and another concerned person to sort it out.

One day I received a phone call from a lady who owned an elderly black cat. She had obtained him from a rescue shelter several years before, where he had been left with a companion cat. The lady had adopted the two of them and had kept them for about five years. Then her circumstances changed and she had to move a distance away and could not take Aubrey with her. Aubrey was not his real name. The other cat had died. So, very sadly, she had contacted me for help. As is often the case, she had left it until the last moment before moving house, and by then there was little time to get Aubrey accommodated, so it became an emergency.

She brought him along one evening and bade him an emotional farewell, leaving me a month's board for his immediate keep, and his inoculation certificate. I installed him in an office pen so that he would have more contact with people coming and going and not feel too isolated. He was a shy little fellow, withdrawn and bewildered, as was to be expected. However, he responded to a bit of fussing and also ate his food, which was good. I thought the best plan was to leave him to settle for a few weeks and then try to find him a home with a single elderly person who would give him all the care and attention he deserved.

This was, I thought, a reasonable course to follow until I thoughtlessly happened to mention Aubrey to a female acquaintance connected with animal welfare, whom I will call Mrs Know-All. Immediately, almost before the words were out of my mouth, she pounced. "Well you can't have him, you've already got three cats [Mimi, Willoughby and Kang]; leave it to me. I know just the couple, their cat's just died, had him for 19 years, they're heartbroken. You would be very selfish to take him. He needs a home on his own!"

I tried to get it through to her that Aubrey was at least 13 and surely the couple would not want a cat of that age and would opt for one much younger. But this was brushed aside as of no consequence and within an hour Mrs Know-All was on the doorstep with a cat basket.

To this day I blame myself for what happened. Because Mrs Know-All seemed so confident that the couple wanted another cat, and had had one before for nineteen years, I assumed it would all work out. I also took to heart the fact that she'd accused me of being selfish by wanting to keep him, and had said that I would not be acting in his best interests. I rang Mrs Know-All several times during the next six months and each time she assured me all was well and that Aubrey had settled in. I did not have the new owners' number, but all the time there was doubt niggling away at the back of my mind.

One day I was in the area and decided to pay a visit and see things for myself. I rang the bell and the man answered. He let me in rather reluctantly and I thought he seemed evasive about letting me see Aubrey for myself. The wife chatted away and said he was such a shy cat and that they used to have difficulty getting him to socialize. In fact, the poor little fellow was hiding underneath her chair all the time.

I left the house, resolving to get Aubrey back, no matter what happened. I could tell it was not working out at all.

The next day I had a phone call from one of the neighbours living near Aubrey's new home. I knew this person from many years back and trusted him. He used to visit the couple frequently and, being a cat lover, had noticed how unhappy the cat was. He had not settled in at all and would have nothing to do with the man. Please Jenny, Phillip pleaded, get him away from there.

So I phoned the couple and heard the true story. It was Mrs Know-All who had more or less talked them into having Aubrey. They had wanted more of a space in between losing their old cat and getting another. They had even considered having a dog this time, which would have suited them better. They hadn't liked to offend Mrs Know-All and hadn't wanted to upset me as I was her friend.

We certainly are not friends, I said emphatically, and lost no time in getting out the car and driving over to bring Aubrey home.

We had trouble trying to persuade him to come out from under the chair. The silly man got down on his knees and tried to drag him out by his front leg. I nearly screamed at him as I could see Aubrey was terrified. He flew out of the room into the kitchen and I was able to get near enough to scoop him up and put him into his original cat carrier. He settled himself in. I think he was so relieved to get away from such a miserable situation. I left without speaking to the couple, drove home and installed Aubrey in the office pen, where he settled into a cat bed with a sigh of relief.

I lost no time in phoning Mrs Know-All and telling her about what had happened. She feigned surprise and said the couple would have been better off with a dog. I said that they ought not to have any pet at all and told her about how the man had mishandled Aubrey in front of me. “How many times had it happened?” I said. She went quiet, and then said “Oh well, he’s all right now you have got him”. I replied that he was certainly not going anywhere else. And that was the last time I spoke to Mrs Know-All!

So his last twilight year was spent in relative peace and calm in the office with Will, Mimi and Kang. They all treated him with consideration; there were no fights and sometimes you would see him sitting shyly at the side of good-natured Mimi. He established his own little routine, staying all day in the office, and then at dusk in the summer months would go out through the cat flap and potter off through the hedge to sit by the next door neighbour’s pond.

We always checked he was in at night and there he would be, sitting in his basket, quiet and content.

In the last twelve months of his life I tried to give him all the care and love that he had missed during those few months of misery and distress. He would rub his old head against my hand, rather like Oliver used to. The third black cat to live here and I thought of Dad, and Mary who had sent Mimi to me.

Aubrey was put to sleep after he developed kidney problems. I did not prolong his life with steroids. I think they give false hope to owners, and in a very old cat it does not seem justified. He is buried in our garden with all the others.

One thing I learned at poor little Aubrey’s expense was to trust my own judgment, and not listen to people like Mrs Know-All.

AUBREY

ETUDE XII : CHIVERS 2004 -

I had always wanted a ginger cat and we had never ever had a kitten before. So here was Chivers, aged 10 weeks, and full of all the self-importance and cheek of a male kitten in its first new home.

He was the last of a litter of four looking for a home. I saw the advertisement and in a moment of madness went and got him. His arrival caused a minor sensation with our two remaining felines, Mimi and Willoughby. Mimi took on the role of surrogate mother and spent endless hours washing him. He submitted to this with good grace and it was comical to watch the look on his naughty face as she administered to his needs. Will was having none of his sauce and didn't hesitate to give him an admonishing smack with his paw if he overstepped the mark.

He is now almost two years old and an extremely handsome animal, marmalade, with pale gold stripes. His paws and chest are white and there is a white area, evenly marked, around his small pink nose.

He charms my customers with his mischievous antics: his favourite trick is to untie shoe laces, but only if they are trainers. Polished leather shoes he leaves alone, for some reason.

He has a special fascination for the taps on the sink and will spend hours licking the bottom of the tap and patting the water as it trickles out. In order to prevent him from becoming bored, we went to the expense of installing a water feature in his play pen. This however, to our chagrin, he totally ignores, always going back to the tap!

We now have just the two cats: Himself, and Mimi. Willoughby passed away about four months after Chivers arrived on the scene.

He is good company for Mimi, and in fact she does get a little bit of exercise when they play together. He loves to hide beneath a chair cover, and then make a sudden dart forward as she rolls past on her way to the feeding dish. There is then a skirmish and she pins him to the floor with a ferocious growl, but they spring apart and the next minute they are sitting together in their basket and she is washing him!

CHIVERS

His curiosity is endless. There is not a cupboard he has not climbed into, a drawer he has not investigated, a window he has not peered into or out of. He has climbed into the washing machine, also the tumble dryer, not when in use of course.

For all his naughty ways it is difficult to be cross with him for long. He breathed new life into Mimi, and I don't think either she or Will would have tolerated a mature cat.

With his looks and charm he could get away with murder!

SOLO

TIGS – THE TIME-SHARE CAT

Tigger, as he was first of all named, did not approve of his new home. His elderly owner had moved into sheltered accommodation and was allowed to have her cat with her. However, Tigger decided the new home was not to his liking, took himself off, and was missing for a month.

His owner was very worried and did not think she would see him again. However, the slender tabby cat with the rather melancholy expression returned to his new home and decided it was probably in his best interests to stay put.

Then misfortune happened: his owner became ill and had to go into hospital for an indefinite period. Fortunately she had good neighbours who looked after Tigger while she made up her mind what to do with him.

Hilda, one of the neighbours, who also boarded her cat Whiskey with me, contacted me after a while and asked if I could find Tigger a home. The owner felt too poorly to cope with a pet and had given permission for Tigger to be re-housed.

This proved to be easier than I had envisaged. Another customer of mine, Maggie, had recently lost one of her cats and the remaining cat, Muffin, was pining for his companion. So Maggie came to see Tigger and decided he was the ideal replacement.

I was quite happy to see him go to his new home. I knew Maggie had owned many cats in her time and understood their different habits. However, it did not work out as we had hoped.

Tigger was a strange old boy, very aloof and wary. You had to let him come to you on his own terms. He was a loner. Although he bonded very well with Muffin, he would not make friends with Maggie, which upset her a great deal. I told her to give him time and he would come to trust her when he was ready. He had had a tremendous upheaval, being moved to another house after five years, going missing, and then coming into my cattery for several weeks, and then another new home to get used to.

Then tragedy struck. Muffin, to whom Tigger was now very devoted, was run over and killed outside Maggie's bungalow. She was devastated and inconsolable. She rang me in floods of tears and there was little I could say to comfort her. I knew all too well what she was experiencing, after the untimely death of our poor Kizzy.

From that day Tigger was a different cat. He refused to have anything more to do with Maggie; it was almost as if he blamed her for what had happened to Muffin. He spent all of his days out of doors, and I believe he was looking for his old friend. He would come home at night just for meals and run away from Maggie if she tried to fuss him. It was all so very sad and I did feel for her. Fate can often deal a cruel blow to those who least deserve it.

After about six months Maggie rang me in a very emotional state asking if I would have Tigger back. She had tried her hardest to win him over but it was just not to be. She missed having the comfort and companionship of a cat on her lap like Muffin. Also, as she loved to travel, it meant she would be free to come and go as she pleased.

It was the middle of August, my busiest time. The only place I could accommodate him in was the storeroom next to the office. He was very stressed and confused and spent most of his time crouched on the window sill behind the refrigerator.

I gave him as much fuss as I could when he would allow me to get near him. But after two weeks I could see he was just craving for his freedom and would have to be released. I had no intention of finding him another home as he was far too traumatised for another owner to get used to. Also he had stopped using his litter tray, which was a major hygiene problem.

So one hot August evening I left the fanlight open and the next morning he had gone. I was not surprised. I knew he would never have settled happily. I left food out for him at the top of the garden each night and it would be gone the next morning.

I placed a cat trap with some food inside one evening and the next morning went up to investigate. Tigger was not inside, but our resident hedgehog was, bumbling round and round in high indignation, after spending the night imprisoned in the trap! The missing food mystery was thus explained.

I advertised his details round the village but had no replies; he could have gone miles away. Hilda, who had told me about him in the first place, kept an eye open for him, in case he had wandered back to his former home. But as the days passed there was no news of his being seen.

I started to worry about him as winter was approaching, although he was not an old cat, and would probably be able to fend for himself. I felt I had failed him. I was convinced he was still looking for his old friend Muffin. I had not contacted Maggie who was on holiday. He may have been trying to get back to that area.

He was in the back of my mind all the time, and then one day, just a few days before Christmas 2004, I received a phone call from Sonia, a friend who lived in the village. She had been feeding a stray tabby cat that had been hovering in the garden for the last few weeks. Her husband Frank thought it was a pregnant female as its stomach was very bloated.

I knew at once it was our Tigger, the fat stomach being due to worms, no doubt, after living rough for four months. I got the car out and went down to Sonia and Frank's bungalow and there was Tigger, gloomily regarding me from under the dining table. "Oh, it's her again" he seemed to be thinking. I had been worrying about him for four months and this was the only thanks I got! Cats are so different from dogs in their affections.

Sonia and Frank had always owned cats but had not got one at present. Did they want Tigger? Not at the moment - they would be away for Christmas - but afterwards perhaps.

So I took him home with me, fully expecting trouble. But to my surprise he settled in at once, glad to have regular good food, a bed to sleep in, and a fussing when he would allow it.

TIGS

Sonia and Frank returned in the New Year, half decided on having him permanently. Then he made up their minds for them by going AWOL again and, after a few days, turning up at their bungalow.

Cats choose where they want to be and both Mistress Minnie Mouser and Tigger were examples of this.

However, I still have contact with Tigs, as he is now renamed. His new owners go away often and so he comes to me frequently for holidays. He is a special guest and resides in the office and storeroom with Mimi and Chivers. Not for him an outside cat pen.

I took him to the vet's once when he had injured his eye and Sam, the young vet, remarked on his proud bearing. A cat I feel privileged to know, she said. He did have a Roman nose, so maybe there was Siamese in his lineage somewhere way back.

Some people have a timeshare apartment; I have a timeshare cat.

DUET -- ROWLEY and SNOWY

Now, two stories of two very different cats:

Rowley, an aristocratic Birman and

Snowy, an abandoned waif

ROWLEY

Margot Collingbourn-Beevers

Rowley was, I think, more intelligent than many humans … and almost frighteningly psychic. He was the most lovable seal point Birman, who came to be rather more my alter-ego than my shadow. From the moment when I first brought him home he was with me all the time, following me around, talking to me, and jumping on my shoulders whenever he had a perch to leap from. In the morning he would see me off to work and in the afternoon or evening he would be waiting for me outside the garage - some fifty yards from our house - no matter what time I arrived home.

Except … that one day he just wasn't waiting there, and his milk was still in his saucer. The previous evening he had been more persistent in his attentions than usual, walking round my shoulders, up in my arms, unsettled in my lap - somehow I felt he was trying to tell me something … something very, very important, that unfortunately I was unable to grasp. Did he really know that some disaster was about to happen, that we were going to lose each other? I believe he did, but what it was that he was trying to communicate I shall sadly never know.

Never again was Rowley ever there for me when I returned home, or when I needed his affection. Enquiries with neighbours and the police, searching walks, phone calls, notices on fences and newspapers - all were tried, but nothing resulted … he was so young, so beautiful, so loving… and then, so suddenly, gone for ever.

How I wish that I'd been able to understand what he was trying to tell me that night, so that I might have been able to save him from whatever evil fate it was that he feared he had to face, and sadly did, in truth, have to face the following day - alone and unprotected.

ROWLEY

in his favourite chair – mine!

SNOWY

Vera Allen (with introduction by Jenny Fensom)

My good friends and near neighbours, Vera and Cliff, used to board their lurcher cross, Boots, with me every year when they and their two young daughters went on holidays. Then they acquired Polly, a small grey kitten from a local rescue centre. She was suffering from cat flu and had had a poor start in life. However, she survived and although she never grew into a large cat, she dominated and terrorised the household, including sweet-natured Boots.

Vera described Polly as a small, unattractive rat-like creature with large watery eyes that would glare balefully at whoever incurred her displeasure. She would suddenly decide she wanted to sit on someone's lap and would leap up and remain there whether it was convenient or not. When the unfortunate member of the family or visitor tried to get up or make to move, Polly would snarl fiercely and pin her victim to the seat, with claws fully extended. This could be quite embarrassing for poor Vera and Cliff, but at least it was a deterrent for keeping unwanted people from calling. (Perhaps every home should own a Polly!)

However, Polly lived to a good age and remained Top Cat in the household, for a great many other felines were to join the family as the years passed.

Helen, an elderly lady who lived opposite Vera, loved animals and kept a number of cats, a dog, a goose and several rabbits in her large garden. Then sadly she died, the pets were all re-homed, and the cats went to live on a farm in the village. However, two of the cats returned to their old home: a mother cat and her ginger and white kitten.

Vera and her neighbour used to feed them but did not encourage them in. Vera now had two other cats belonging to her daughter, and the infamous Polly, who would not allow the cats over the threshold. Also there was another stray named Blackie that paid frequent visits to the house. Eventually the mother cat was run over outside on the busy road and poor little Snowy, as Vera christened him, was now an orphan.

Vera, in her own words, tells the story of Snowy:

Snowy came into our lives, unloved and unwanted. Orphaned as a kitten, he spent years living under a hedge, fed by a neighbour. He often came and peered hopefully through our cat flap like a little phantom, but our resident cats said "SCRAM" – the top cat Polly was so ferocious that she guarded the house like a rottweiler! I often said 'hello' to Snowy and offered him a small titbit, but initially he was too scared to take it from my hand. Eventually he would tap me gently, take the scrap and run off.

As each of our cats got old and died he was convinced his turn had come. So we gave in, with slightly bad grace. He immediately made himself one of the family, and rewarded us during his remaining years with total love and many gifts, in spite of having only two teeth!

I often regret those lost years, but maybe he had perfect timing. I cried when he died suddenly, one hot August Sunday.

SNOWY finds comfort at last

INTERLUDE - *The Picture Gallery*

CHIVERS and WILLOUGHBY
a few days before Willoughby died

His Imperial Highness Chocolate Point Siamese KANG

CHIVERS at four months old

MINNIE playing peek a boo

BAG PUSS goes to school

KIZZY

WORDSWORTH

TRIO

HARRY BAKER, THE VEGETARIAN CAT

SIM, THE ENGINE CAT

TOOTS, THE TOOTER CAT

HARRY THE VEGETARIAN CAT

Pat and Martin Baker (with introduction by Jenny Fensom)

My friends Pat and Martyn Baker have owned a variety of cats over the years. They have been regular customers at Good Companions and their two sons, Nick and Tim, also are great cat lovers.

The first cat of theirs that I remember coming to stay was a black and white male named Rudi. There was also an aristocratic Russian Blue, whom the family named Boris, and who had simply arrived on their doorstep one day. However, in typical cat-like fashion he decided he would rather live with an elderly couple living nearby, who always had a hot cooked lunch every day! The Baker family however felt quite honoured by the fact that they were even considered to be suitable candidates for Boris's favours.

There have been other cats since him, but the current cat in the Baker residence is Harry, a sweet-natured feline now aged 12.

In their own words Pat and Martyn tell the story of Harry:

Back in 1995 we visited a Luton cat refuge, and brought home a frightened black and white kitten, who promptly hid in the vegetable rack in the kitchen, and made it her home.

Having just returned from a holiday in France, we decided to call her "Harry" short for "haricot verts" - as she was clearly very much at home with vegetables!

She grew into a lovely, placid and affectionate cat, though she panics completely whenever the dustbin lorry comes, or when we put out the bins. We suspect that she was part of a litter that was thrown away into a wheelie bin and rescued by the dustmen all those years ago. Harry is now nearly 12 years old. We still spend our holidays in France, so Harry enjoys a long summer break with Jenny at "Good Companions" each year.

However, through the cold winter months she stays snug and warm at home, and can usually be found stretched out asleep along the top of the radiator in the living room. A very contented and a very hot cat!

Down in Devon, our son Nick also has a cat. "Brock" is lean, agile and completely black. His full name is "Broccoli", following in the Baker family tradition of naming our cats after green vegetables ... !

HARRY

SIM THE ENGINE CAT

A tale of Rachel Gough's cat (told by Jenny Fensom)

One Bonfire Night animal lover Rachel Gough went into her back garden to cover up her rabbit hutches. Suddenly she heard a faint mewing coming from under one of the hutches. She looked underneath and, crouching there, was a tiny ginger kitten barely six weeks old. His eyes were still blue; goodness knows where he had come from.

So Rachel kept the tiny creature and named him Simba, which later got shortened to Sim because Rachel's young daughter Danielle could only lisp "Sim" at the time.

He grew into a handsome cat, very placid in nature and easy to handle.

However, some years ago he had a fur-raising experience but lived to tell the tale. Rachel's partner, Darren, was driving to Aylesbury, which is about 15 miles from their home in Luton. He stopped halfway at a garage to get a drink of pop, and just as he was starting the engine he heard a mewing from under the bonnet.

On investigating he found, to his horror, poor Sim curled up on the engine, looking dazed and bewildered. Immediately Darren turned the car round and, with Sim on his lap, headed straight back to the vet in Dunstable. Apart from singed whiskers and of course the shock, the vet pronounced Sim unhurt; he had had an amazing escape.

After this incident, which could easily have ended in tragedy, the car is checked very carefully before any journey!

Sim is now a sedate eleven-year-old, and a regular visitor to my cattery. He is always accompanied by his little orange, cuddly cat toy from which he refuses to be parted.

SIM

Rachel tells me that her much-loved cat objects to people sneezing and miaows loudly in disapproval. Also, for some reason, he always insists on eating his Sunday lunch with the family in the dining room, instead of in his usual place in the kitchen.

He is obviously a cat capable of showing great stoicism under stress and of very traditional tastes and predictable in his habits. If ever the day should dawn when cats took over this country and ruled us, I think he would make a superb Prime Minister ...

TOOTS THE TOOTER CAT

Rhona French, aged 11

I glance across at the light pink tongue washing sleek black fur. Two emerald eyes blink at me and then turn away to continue with washing.

I think of how we got him. I can't remember because I wasn't alive then, but I feel as if I was there, since I've heard the tale so many times before ...

Toots came to Mum and Dad. They didn't buy him: he just appeared outside. Oh, they tried everything to get him to go back home; posters, not feeding him, for example, but he was determined to stay put, so they fed him.

I always like to think that I have a special connection with Toots since his name was my first word and I usually feed him. But he means everything to all of us, Mum, Dad, my brother and me. This is proved by choruses of song singing his praises late at night.

However, Toots' affection is also for food. He adores it so much that he can lick it off a spoon standing on his hind legs.

Toots stares at me (he's now finished with washing) pleading for ... you've guessed it ... food.

Oh Toots, please stay with us for many more years ... we might even make up a new song about you!

Jenny Fensom adds:

Rhona is our youngest contributor to Cat Etudes.

Her parents, Joe and Annette, have been customers of mine since 1991.

Toots appeared on their doorstep one day, aged about 10 months, and has been the much-loved family cat ever since.

He has a lovely placid disposition and I always enjoy having him to stay at Good Companions for his yearly holidays.

TOOTS

QUARTET

Contributed by members of Sidmouth Poetry Readers

SAMMY - *Beryl Smyter*

KITTEN VERSUS OLD HAND - *Judy Ritz*

MY CONTENTED CAT - *Stewart Gordon*

KITTEN SPRING - *Margot Collingbourn-Beevers*

The next four contributions are from members of Sidmouth Poetry Readers:

BERYL pays an affectionate tribute to her much loved pet cat, Sammy

JUDY gives an amusing description of the mischievous antics of the two young kittens living on one side of her house, contrasting these with the dignified and indifferent attitude of the elderly tom on the other side

STEWART has based his poem on the true story of a soldier smuggling a dog back from a foreign land

MARGOT has likened the long-awaited arrival of Spring to the awakening curiosity of a very young inquisitive kitten

SAMMY

Beryl Smyter

Sammy's at his tricks again
He thinks I cannot see
But I keep an eye on him
Whilst I sip my tea.

He's sitting by the armchair
I know he wants to leap
Because his gaze goes upwards
Then down below the seat.

There are some dangling grasses
With daffodils on show
If I don't go and move them
His paw will, with one blow.

One cannot rest a minute
When that Sammy is in sight
He patrols around the hallway
To see each door shut tight.

His favourite room the kitchen
We caught him on the brink
Diving down a little hole
Underneath the sink.

He came up later eyes awide
Whiskers draped in a web
With a mouse between his teeth
A present for me he said.

Sometimes I want to cuddle
This fluffy ginger tom
But when I go to pick him up
He's off like a whizzing bomb

I try my hardest to adore him
When he purrs and looks all sweet
But once he's had his dinner,
Sam's off to bed, to sleep.

SAMMY

KITTENS VERSUS OLD HAND

Judy Ritz

Cautious polka-dot kitten
Perches on wisteria,
Ponders possibility of
Precarious leap to
Combat ginger tom…
Perhaps not!

Purring pussy
Pirouettes around his tail,
Strolls nonchalantly through
Rose garden and leaps
Into bird bath,
Scattering water.

Uninvited sleek, black
Jet propelled puss
Streaks through cat-flap
To consume
Tom's supper!

But cat of certain age
Is unperturbed
By naughtiness,
Haughtiness is the key.
He simply sits, aloof,
Contemplating
Two balls of fluffy nonsense.

A CONTENTED CAT

Stewart Gordon

I often take Jamie, my tiger, for a walk
Along the Sidmouth Byes,
And should we meet another cat
He seldom shows surprise.
But there are some dogs who skulk away,
Whilst other rush past us rather rapidly,
Although my own two dogs remain and stay.
The people have always stood and gazed
And not believed their eyes,
For they are just amazed to see a tiger
Walking down the Byes.
They marvel at his noble head and amber eyes,
The black and orange stripes of his disguise,
The strength, and power of his limbs - his size.
For all in all he is majestical.
And this magnificence they will relate
To their children and grandchildren
At some later date. Jamie was born in India,
Where a member of his family had been shot by Royalty,
Under the false impression that
They were more royal than he.
So I brought him home with me
Although he was just a cub,
Away from all that danger, turmoil
And general hubbub.
He travelled at the bottom of my old kit bag,
Where he sat quietly and was as good as gold,
For he was an illegal immigrant
If the truth were told.

And so by troopship we left that foreign land,
And now Jamie much prefers
Sidmouth and the Byes
With all its hinterland.
He loves especially a stroll through Hogsweed Wood
And to take a dip in the River Sid.
That is what he likes to do
So that is what he did.

After his swim he thoroughly shakes his fur,
For like any other cat he is particular.
At night he sleeps with me
Upon my super king-sized bed,
Jamie at my feet my two dogs at my head.
We have no fear of trespass
Or even burglary,
But sleep there altogether
Quite contentedly.
For as I've always said,
"There's nothing so contented
As a contented dog
Sleeping contentedly upon my bed."
And now I have to add to that
The sheer contentment
Of one contented cat.

KITTEN SPRING

Margot Collingbourn-Beevers

Spring Leap

Spring jumped, so unexpectedly, into my lap
like a small and softly purring kitten.
Quite suddenly it came, licking the frosts,
lapping up the later flaking snows;
clawing its way up the spikey barren hedge,
gently softening up the winter harshness
with the fresh young warmth of its gentle breath,
the playful touch of its powerful paw.

Cat Fall

Spring, weakened now by summer's burning sun,
grew thin and shadowed in the heat.
And, outclassed now by boldened June's richesse,
hid tints of pale beneath his fur;
crept sadly to his outcast winter bed,
unheeded there, in full year sleep.
But ... stored within his resting springcome paws
his garden secrets of the resurrection.

QUINTET

Jenny Fensom and Cynthia Mayles write about …

CYNTHIA'S CATS

<><><><>

MOLLY • SKIMBLESHANKS • TOM-TOM

TINKERBELL AND TIGERLILY

MOLLY

My friends Cynthia and Maurice Mayles have boarded their small black cat Molly with me for many years. Molly is very much her own puss and extremely choosey about her accommodation at the cattery.

If she does not get the pen she prefers, she makes her displeasure very evident in a way which I won't go into. Suffice it to say that after experiencing Molly's deeds when she is in the wrong pen, I make certain she always has her favourite pen away from the other cats. Rather like a prim, elderly spinster on holiday at her usual hotel, or Greta Garbo herself, Molly likes to be alone. I think she may have Siamese way back in her ancestry.

MOLLY

SKIMBLESHANKS

Cynthia and Maurice owned another cat called Skimbleshanks before Miss Molly came to live with them.

Skinny, for short, was named after Skimbleshanks, one of the cats from Andrew Lloyd Webber's show "CATS".

Cynthia recalls:

We collected her from a rescue home. She was a joy to have and didn't travel far from either our back or front gardens. We nearly lost her once when an over-zealous youngster proceeded to carry her off! I quickly rescued her. She ended her days with us and sadly had to be put to sleep at about fourteen.

A loving, dear friend to the last.

SKIMBLESHANKS

TOM-TOM

Cynthia, in her own words, relates the story of a further cat, one she befriended called Tom-Tom:

One fine spring day, a handsome ginger fellow came to our garden. I offered him a little something, and that was it. Very timid, but so polite, a saucer of milk brought an instant "Miaow!" of thanks. I thought he probably lived nearby on our estate.

On arrival back from our holidays, the following morning an almighty howling could be heard. Yes, you've guessed it. It was Ginge, as I called him, ready for some food.

I then realised that he must be a stray, as he rarely left our garden. So grateful for anything going.

Now, here was the problem. Molly, our rescued cat, did not take to Ginge at all.

I put cards in shop windows, asked around the district - nothing! I took him to our vet to see if he had been chipped. He hadn't, but he had been neutered. However, there was a missing cat reported to our vet.

On phoning, a distressed lady explained that "Tom" had gone missing some six weeks ago, when they had moved to St Albans. Already she had been to see six cats that were not "Tom."

She came to see him but, as I had just brought him back from the vet, he wouldn't emerge from the bushes at the back of our garden. Then she caught sight of him.

"Ooh, that's Tom!" she cried, quite tearfully. I said: "Here's some biscuits, call him, he'll know you!"

Tom wasn't having any of this and he crept back into the bushes.

"Never mind," I said. "We'll get him in the morning when he comes for breakfast."

Next morning, very happy, the lady came for Tom, bearing a lovely bunch of flowers and two bottles of wine.

"Many thanks," I said, and rather sadly said good bye to Tom.

Very excited, the lady went back with Tom to be reunited with his owner, her partner. Later that evening a nice young man phoned with many thanks for looking after Tom.

"Just one small thing" he said. "It's not Tom, but do you mind if we keep him?"

I was delighted to have found this gorgeous cat a loving home, after all that. I missed Tom-Tom quite a lot, and renamed him after the original cat.

TOM-TOM

TINKERBELL AND TIGERLILY

The Mayles family's love of cats extends to the third generation. Cynthia's son and daughter-in-law were looking for two kittens for their two daughters, Charlotte and Bethany.

One evening Cynthia rang me and asked if I knew if there were any available.

As it happened I did know of someone whose cat had recently had a litter, so I gave Cynthia the number.

It is strange how often in life fate steps in and lends a hand. Within half an hour of the phone call, I had another call from my good friend and fellow cat-lover Vera, who lives close by. Vera was very worried about two young cats whose owners were splitting up and had, urgently, to find homes for Tinkerbell and

Tigerlily, two litter sisters who needed to stay together.

I rang Cynthia back and asked if her son would consider two adult cats for his daughters, instead of kittens. The cats were so pretty, tortoiseshell and white with sweet faces. So the Mayles family went to see the cats and came home with them. It's not often that rescued cats get sorted out so quickly and easily. It was as if it was all meant to be.

So I have these two lovely tortoiseshell princesses to stay in my cattery at holiday times and they are as sweet natured as they look.

TIGERLILY

TINKERBELL

NONET

NINE LIVES *Manuel Martins*

Jenny writes: *My friend and lover of cats, Manuel Martins, talks to me about the cats he has owned over the forty years he has lived in Sidmouth, Devon.*

Manuel recalls:

My first cat was a tiny black and white male kitten that I bought for five shillings in 1971 from a lady selling refreshments in a kiosk at Peak Hill car park. The poor little creature was suffering from cat flu and I didn't think he would survive, but he did and grew into a large, handsome cat. I named him Ben.

After a few years he went missing for several weeks; I was very upset and gave up all hope of seeing him again.

There was a litter of kittens born in the grounds of the hotel where I worked, so one day I brought two little black sisters home with me. I called them Lucy and Sweet Fanny Adams. They settled down well, and then one day, to my joy and surprise, who should walk into the kitchen, but long lost Ben! He had a hip injury. I expect he had been hit by a car a long way from home and had slowly, over the weeks, made his way back.

How would the three cats get along together?

The two kittens loved Ben from the start and would snuggle up at the side of him as if he was their own mother. He was very gentle and tolerant towards them and they were all happy together.

This lasted for about a year and then one day I went out into the garden and Ben lay dead on the compost heap. He must have suffered an internal injury from his accident and had died as a result.

I was very upset, and Lucy and Sweet Fanny Adams missed their adopted 'mother'.

LUCY and SWEET FANNY ADAMS

My next cat to arrive was Daisy, a beautiful tortoiseshell. She eventually had a litter of four kittens and I kept two of them, Honey and Rose. While she was nursing them she would not let Lucy and Fanny Adams near them. She was like a miniature lioness defending her cubs! Fanny Adams disappeared and went to live on some nearby allotments and did not return until the kittens were weaned.

Some while later I took on another cat from a man who was moving into a place where pets were not allowed. I named her Papaya. She was beautiful, ginger and fluffy.

HONEY

Most of my cats, except Ben, lived to a great age. Lucy and Fanny Adams, 17 and 20; Papaya and Honey also 17.

My last two cats were LC and Tuna. Poor little LC was living rough in the grounds of the hotel. No one seemed to own her, so I brought her home with me. She was grey and white in colour.

I did not have her for very long; I think she was about eight and became very ill with a lung condition, and in the end I had to have her put to sleep.

My present cat is a black and white female called Tuna, who belonged to a colleague of mine, Graham, who went to work on the liner Queen Mary II.

Of course Tuna could not go with Graham so he asked me if I would have her. I was still feeling sad about losing LC, but Tuna was so friendly, loving and intelligent that I could not resist her.

So she is well settled into my house, loves meeting people and even has been known to 'talk' to them on the phone.

I love the names Manuel chose for his nine cats. I wonder whether he was inspired and influenced by his native beautiful country of Madeira, the island of sunshine and warmth, fruit and flowers.

I asked him what LC stood for (I thought he meant Elsie at first). "Lost Cat, of course!" he said, surprised that I had not guessed.

And what about Sweet Fanny Adams? He just gave me an enigmatic grin!

TUNA

NOCTURNES

RONNIE - *Jenny Fensom*

TIGGER WESTFIELD - *Jenny Fensom*

WHISKY ONE AND WHISKY TWO - *Eileen and Bill Reay*

TOM - *Paul Betts*

Old Deuteronomy's lived a long time;
He's a Cat who has lived many lives in succession.

Old Possum's Book of Practical Cats   T S ELIOT

I have always had a respect and admiration for elderly cats. I have several that have been boarding at my cattery every year for the last 16 years or so. Here are just a few fond tributes to some of my special geriatric cats.

RONNIE

Ronnie came to me for his holidays for the first time two years ago. Then, aged 15, it was the first time he had ever been in a cattery.

A faded ginger and white, he arrived in a basket tied up with string. He was blind in one eye, but the other one, I noticed, missed nothing. He was giving both me and his new environment a very shrewd appraisal!

I decided he would be better off in a storeroom pen, near to the house so that I could pop in more often and keep an eye on him. I am always anxious with very aged cats as they can be more open to infection than their younger brethren, or may of course pine for their owners if it is the first time they have ever been left.

Mister Ronnie, however, made it clear that from the start that he was going to have things his way. His lady owner chuckled as she left him and said mysteriously that Ronnie had once had an identical twin brother, also ginger and white.

"We called him Reggie," she said, as she got into her car. Being rather slow on the uptake these days, the penny took a long while to drop, until later that evening when I went to check Ronnie.

His pen was in chaos, his litter tray overturned, water from his drinking bowl swimming everywhere, and his bedding shredded. Ronnie was standing on his hind legs growling ferociously, his good eye glinting fire and defiance, his bad one sinister and threatening.

Tigs, who happened to be staying at that time, was perched on the window sill looking out, ignoring the pandemonium that was going on.

I put Ronnie into another pen, settled him for the night, and left him with some of his favourite food. I heard an angry hiss as I closed the door and the unmistakable clank of a feeding bowl being overturned. He was only booked in for one week, but it was going to be a very long week!

Anti-social humans these days are given ASBOs; Ronnie and his late brother Reggie, I decided, needed ASPURRS.

The next day I went to the storeroom expecting the worst as it was so quiet. That was suspicious in itself. I opened the door and cautiously looked in and saw to my horror that the pen was empty.

The door was open and Tigs was sitting sphinx-like on the window sill with both paws tucked under him. He threw me a casual look as if to say, "Don't worry, everything is under control, I've sorted it all out". There are some cats, and Tigs is one of them, who always make me feel so inadequate.

I searched the room frantically for Ronnie and there he was, sitting smugly in a cardboard box on the floor, completely relaxed and in control of the situation.

I concluded that Tigs had undone the pen somehow and had released Ronnie. He had always bonded well with other cats and perhaps Ronnie had reminded him of long lost Muffin, the cat he had loved so much.

So Ronnie spent his week's holiday settled in his box, eating soft mushy food as he had few teeth left. Tigs kept a brotherly eye on him and I marvelled again at the strange empathy that exists between animals, and how much wiser they are than us mere humans. We have so much to learn from them.

NB - Ronnie is the only cat featured in this book whose owners did not wish to be identified (for obvious reasons).

There is a mug shot of Ronnie at the FDB (FELINE DELINQUENT BUREAU).

His late brother Reggie is also featured and, of course, Millwall from an earlier chapter of this book, and Polly, the Rottweiler cat belonging to Vera. (see Chapter 'SNOWY').

TIGGER WESTFIELD

He was born in 1991 and was one of two remaining kittens in a litter. He had a funny kink in the end of his tail and this was probably an old injury from birth. When he was only 6 months old he was run over and lost the sight of one eye.

He has been a long standing guest at my cattery and is now aged 15.

He usually has the same pen and when it is feeding time he puts on quite a performance if he is not fed first. He continually strikes the wire on his pen, and mews in a very authoritative tone. A typical elderly gentleman getting impatient if the service at the hotel is not up to standard!

Tigger's owner, Wendy Westfield, tells me that he is afraid of nothing, and all of the dogs in the neighbourhood cross the road when they see Tigger sitting outside on the pavement! Whatever the size, Tigger will give chase and see them off his territory.

I wonder if Ron and Reggie were his litter siblings; they were all the same colour and age!

TIGGER

WHISKY ONE and WHISKY TWO

THE FULL STORY IN BLACK AND WHITE *Bill and Eileen Reay*

It all began 37 years ago with a stroll down Petticoat Lane Market in London one Sunday, not intending to buy anything.

As it was nearing closing time we thought we would take our son, then aged 2, to the animal market just up the road from there. There was not a lot to see but we happened to pass a cage with a tiny black and white kitten in the corner on its own. Of course we stopped and aarh-ed at how cute it was and, before we knew it, the stall-holder had pounced! "What do you want, a Tom?" he said. We didn't say anything. He then picked it up, lifted its tail, said "It's a Tom" and we handed over 50p. My, how times have changed!

As we had had no intention of buying a pet of any kind, we then had to work out how we were going to get it home on the underground. We held Whisky - that's what we named him - very close to us but he decided he would much rather sit on Bill's shoulder all the way back to Hendon. The following morning we took him to the PDSA (again on Bill's shoulder) to get him checked out and the Vet told us off for buying him at a market and said he would never last. He also told us that our Tom was in fact a She! She never needed to visit a Vet again, apart from her annual injections. We gave her a very good life and she gave us plenty of love, and 17 years later she died of a stroke.

We missed her so much that we immediately went looking for Whisky II. A friend's cat had just had kittens, and we found one that was also black and white. At this time we also decided to get a bearded collie dog, whom we named Charlie. Whisky was not very impressed with him at the start and kept growling at him. As Charlie had cost us a lot of money, I thought we would have to send Whisky back from whence she came. It did not take long, however, before they became the best of friends and inseparable, with Whisky even coming on walks with us, following us up the road.

Both Whisky and Charlie emigrated to Perth, Australia, when they were 2 years old, spending 2 months in quarantine there. Whisky loved the heat and insects and often came in with a fat lip where something or other had bitten her. We didn't enjoy the heat but if ever we came home in the car, she would immediately sit on the bonnet and get extra heat from the engine – how she was never bar-b-q'd I do not know.

We returned to England when they were 8 years old, and this time it was 6 months in quarantine. I think it was harder for us than for them but we all survived. Whisky was not too happy about returning to the cold and even now sits on our laps until the chair is warm enough and then pushes us off. She is definitely the 'boss' of the house. After eating she wanders into the living room and wipes her face on our slippers, then wants a warm lap. She is not frightened of dogs - just gives them her 'evil stare' and stays put while they back away.

She very rarely visits the Vet but in November 2005 we got worried as she was not eating or drinking. The Vet gave her the usual blood tests and we were told that her kidneys and pancreas were packing up and that, because of her age (19), there was nothing they could do. We prepared ourselves for the worst and decided to 'do the deed'. She must have known what was on our minds because she perked up, started eating us out of house and home, and is now looking forward to her 20th birthday in August 2006.

WHISKY NUMBER I

WHISKY NUMBER II

TOM

Paul Betts

Jenny writes: *Last summer I had a very distinguished elderly gentleman tabby staying at Good Companions for a month. The cat in question was Tom, our cousin Paul's cat, aged 18.*

Paul in his own words gives an account of Tom's long life:

Tom was a great cat, and good friend and companion to all our family.

I remember when we were living at Dropshort Cottage, Great Gaddesden, we were asked if we wanted one of our neighbour's kittens. Mum had recently lost her cat on the road outside and said she did not want another cat.

But I went next door and picked Tom: he was so bright and playful. A light tabby grey, like a little tiger. When she saw him, Mum changed her mind, and Tom was her companion for many years. Living in the country, he would sometimes get into her bad books by bringing home mice, sometimes letting them go into the house! Later he moved with Mum to Tring, and loved to sit on her lap, or lie in the sunshine on the window sill.

Sadly, eventually Mum passed away, and Tom moved in with us. He was a real character, and would follow Tracey, Sam and me to the local shops along a safe path and wait outside, among some bushes, until we had finished shopping, and then follow us home, like a faithful dog.

When we moved to the Isle of Wight, Tom spent a month in Jenny's cattery, until the house move was finalised.

Then Tom had a real adventure, when I collected him to bring him to the Island. First, by car to the station, then train to King's Cross, taxi to Waterloo, and train to Portsmouth. He loved all the attention from the other passengers and the guard, on the mainline trains. Then came the ferry crossing to the Island by ... what else but the Fastcat catamaran!

He settled in well by the sea and enjoyed his new environment for about nine months. Then sadly his kidneys failed and the grand old-timer passed away, aged 19, in April of this year, after living a long, happy and full life.

TOM

BAGATELLES *Jenny Fensom*

PERKINS : JOY AND ROLFE

CLAUDE AND SKINNER : CAT LIGHT MANIPULATION

PERKINS

The first cat I ever remember was Perkins, a fluffy tortoiseshell belonging to our neighbours, the Scanes family. I was always asked to feed Perkins when the family went on holiday. I can recall crossing over the road to the large rambling house where the Scanes lived, with all the grave importance of a six-year-old girl, performing her first responsible task.

In post-war Britain there were not many brands of cat food to choose for one's pet. Tins of Kit-e-Kat would be left out, shocking pink in colour and which smelt revolting when you opened the tin. I think I had to have assistance with this: there were no ring-pull cans around at that time. There were pilchards in tomato sauce which Perkins really enjoyed. Also bread and marmite were included; I have never before or since known a cat to be fed on that, but Perkins flourished well on it!

So this was the very first pet minding job I ever had and I remember to this day how seriously I undertook the responsibility!

JOY AND ROLFE

We moved to our present address in 1961. I was aged 12 and had to leave behind all the friends I had made since starting school at the age of five. It was not an easy time, and it was very difficult for me to pick up the threads of life in the new school, set in a large village, and form another circle of friends, so different in outlook and personality, from the girls I had been brought up with in Leagrave, a suburb of Luton.

However, there were compensations. In the village where I lived there was a middle-aged couple, Joy and Rolfe, who were responsible for setting me on the path of caring for pets while their owners went on holiday.

Joy ran a kennels and cattery in her back garden: it was before the days of planning permission and licensing became law. The dogs were kept in small individual kennels. The garden was divided into two and Joy looked after the larger breeds at one end, and Rolfe had the small dogs at the bottom of the garden.

Rolfe was quite a character in his own right. He was of Swiss nationality and very clever. He taught foreign languages at the local college and was fluent in about eight or nine.

Sometimes his different pupils would visit Long Thatch, as the cottage was named, and take tea with us, and I, aged twelve at the time, would listen in, fascinated at the animated conversations, as Rolfe switched from one language to another, whilst chatting in turn to the different students.

He could also be very absent minded. He was about 20 years older than Joy, who was a very attractive woman. She had blonde hair and a kindly, laughing face with lively, twinkling blue eyes. The couple was childless, so all of Joy's maternal love was channelled into the corgis that she bred.

Rolfe loved classical music and often you would hear his gramophone records being played at their loudest when you walked past the garden. During the summer months he slept in a tiny single-berth caravan in the garden and there would be several small kennels with a dog inside each one, housed in the caravan.

I shall never forget the day when he thought one of the dogs was missing and went up the road looking for it. Joy and I were coming back from the village store and saw him standing with his hands shading his eyes scanning the fields opposite. I didn't realize at first what had happened but poor Joy, being long acquainted with her husband's forgetfulness, immediately started to upbraid him the length of the village street. She was a rather highly-strung lady, a great worrier and very sensitive.

"Which dog is it?" Joy demanded, her voice rising to a high pitch.

"That little black mongrel that came yesterday." Rolfe replied, sheepishly.

"I knew that dog would give trouble." Joy moaned. "The sort of ordinary-looking dog that you don't miss until it's gone!"

"What on earth do you mean?" Rolfe observed. "You're not making sense!"

"Don't start to analyse what I've said" snapped Joyce. "Jenny would know what I mean, she's a woman! This is all your fault, listening to those records, you're in a different world".

"We shall be sued!" she continued, over and over, when we got back indoors.

She completely went to pieces, collapsing into an armchair in the small kitchen, as Rolfe, puffing placidly at his habitual cigar, and I searched the garden, nooks and crannies.

Wagner was blaring out on the gramophone, the ideal background music for the occasion!

Then I went and looked in the caravan and there was missing pooch, fast asleep on the bunk! It had been there all the time, just fancied a snooze! "Thank God for you, Jenny", Joy praised me, over and over on that occasion, and poor Rolfe was in the dog-house, as it were, for the rest of the week!

So, that was how it all began as I knocked at the door one July morning, just as the summer holidays began. I was bored to death with nothing to do. I asked if they wanted any help with the dogs. I had only seen Joy once before, being towed up the road by a large, lively, Afghan Hound.

After a few questions she seemed, suddenly, to make up her mind. She led me round to the back of the cottage to where there was a medium-sized wooden shed. Inside there were about 15 cages, 3 foot square, each containing a cat. They were all different colours, some sitting calm and content, others mewing away for attention. She asked me if I would sit inside the shed and let the cats out one at a time for exercise. So this was my first job. I was soon promoted to other tasks, emptying litter trays and refilling with sawdust, feeding the cats and helping with the dogs.

I formed quite a bond with Joy and Rolfe over the three summers that I worked there. They were so interesting to talk to, had travelled to many countries and had a lovely open-minded outlook on life.

Joy was artistic, painted water colours, and also wrote amusing articles which she read out at the local WI meetings. One of the more conventionally-minded lady members once dryly remarked that Joy could get away with murder.

I worked there for three summers in the early 60's. They trusted me to look after a few pets when they went on their school trips and I had a lot of responsibility.

Then, to my dismay, Joy told me one day that they were moving to Yorkshire. Rolfe had taken a better salaried position in a university and wanted to make big life changes. In fact, the cottage they bought was in Hawksworth near Guisley. It was called Windyridge and the lady whom they bought it from had written a well-known book about her life there.

So then Joy suggested to me that I carried on the kennels and cattery from my home, with the goodwill from her clientele. I was only 15 and had no idea of what I really wanted to do except that it must be work with animals.

I was not clever and dedicated enough to study for a veterinary surgeon, far too lazy and undisciplined to apply myself to academic studies. So it came to be that my father, who was a builder, built my kennels and cattery at the top of our large garden. Many of Joy's customers came to me. They knew me well, and were delighted to think someone they could trust would be caring for their pets.

CLAUDE AND SKINNER

Several years ago I received a strange phone call from a man with a strong Irish accent. "Is that the cattery?" he demanded loudly. On replying that it was, he went on in the same loud interrogative manner. "Do you only take pedigree cats?" I said that I accepted both pedigree and non pedigree cats. There was a short pause, then: "Would it be that you make more fuss of the pedigree cats than you do the moggies?".

I was getting a bit annoyed and suspicious at this point. I often received odd phone calls from people, often with absolutely no intention of boarding their cats, just timewasters with nothing better to do. It's the price one pays for being in business, your phone number has to be available, and you become quite vulnerable.

So I replied rather tartly that all the cats that came to stay at Good Companions received the same care, fuss and attention whether they were pedigree, non-pedigree or whatever. This seemed to satisfy him and with a gruff "HUMPH!" and a good-bye he rang off.

I thought no more of it: it was coming up to Christmas and I was beginning to take a lot of bookings. Some were my regular customers of many years, and others were new to the cattery.

It was the day before Christmas Eve and I was waiting for two new cats to come in. They were called Claude and Skinner. I forget the name of the owner under whose name they were booked. Eventually the door bell rang and on the door step stood a very tall man and a lady, presumably his wife. They had two cats in separate baskets, one black (Skinner) and the other ginger (Claude).

I led the way up the garden to the cattery and installed the cats into one of the pens. They each had a large green armchair cushion to sit on, which they had brought with them. I was handed their certificates and then the lady gave me a parcel wrapped up in Christmas paper. "Here's a few chocolates from their owner." She smiled as she handed them over. I thanked her and then remarked that I thought the cats belonged to her and her husband.

The man then shook his head and laughed. "Oh no, I'm just the chauffeur! This is my wife, but Claude and Skinner belong to Peter O' Toole. They were booked in under our name".

It was the biggest surprise that I had ever had. The phone call I had received a few weeks before had been from the great actor himself, checking up on my suitability for looking after his beloved pets. As I found out later, the London cattery, where he used to board Claude and Skinner, had closed down and he needed somewhere near to his London address to board them. His chauffeur, Tom, was Luton based and a friend of Katherine Benny, one of my customers.

She had recommended me and that was how it came about.

I looked after them several times over the years. I never met the great man himself. His agent, Lucy Villiers, used to make the bookings by phone, and Tom always delivered the cats. I would always be presented with a bottle as a special 'thank you' from the two cats.

My brother and I went to see Peter O'Toole in the well-known play: "Jeffery Barnard is Unwell." I bought a programme and, when I saw Tom the next time he brought the cats over, I gave it to him and asked if it could be autographed. He took it with him and later it was sent back to me with the dedication:

"To Jenny Fensom,
who gives digs
to Claude and Skinner
when they take their
holidays.

Love
Peter O'Toole"

Jeffrey Bernard is Unwell
THE OLD VIC

CAT LIGHT MANIPULATION

How to mess up the arrangements and avoid going into a cattery when your owners are off on holiday.

Written by Typhoo, a Siamese cat with more than average intelligence.

“Oh yes, it’s that time of year again. Suitcases brought down from the loft and, most significant, my cat basket being got out from the cupboard under the stairs. She’s just back from the hairdresser and he’s on the drive cleaning the car. The kids are running riot, which isn’t unusual, and here comes our Keith from next door for instructions about watering the plants and feeding the koi carp. He’s wearing his ‘I’m in charge!’ cap; that’s bad news for a start!

“Listen to them all, laughing and happy, very chummy indeed! I’ll soon alter that.

“Now he’s showing Keith some new-fangled contraption on his car. Satellite navigation or some such thing. You can bet Keith’ll be off to Milton Keynes tomorrow to get one for himself: they all have to keep up with one another round here. Copycats!

“The old misery the other side has just banged the fence and says there’s too much noise. I’ll go and dig up all the plants in his garden tonight when they’ve given up looking for me and gone to bed. Because one thing is for certain: I’m not going to the cattery while they go off on holiday and enjoy themselves. Not likely. I’m going to have the time of my life living free for two weeks.

“Now they can’t find my certificate. Panic stations. He says it’s in her handbag; she says he put it in the desk. It’s not in either place; I found it the other day and hid it in the ditch in the sports field. I’m not silly!

“Now they are both arguing and blaming each other. The kids are over-excited and are starting to cry. The dog’s barking and old misery is banging again. It’s all right for the dog, he goes everywhere with them.

“I’ll climb up next door’s tree and watch from there: human beings can be so entertaining and amusing when things go wrong. Oh look! The two tabby cats from over the road are watching from the top of their shed; word’s getting round.

“He’s tripped over the garden hose. What language! Now they are testing the burglar alarm; Keith’s dialled the wrong code and it won’t stop. Old misery has just shouted and said it’s like World War 3 living next to us!

“There goes the phone - I bet it’s the poor woman from the cattery phoning to ask if they are bringing me tonight, as it’s nine o’clock, she’s exhausted and wants to go to bed. They start to call my name: ‘TYPHOO! TYPHOO!’

"I ask you, fancy being saddled with a name like that! Why can't it be something dignified like Marmaduke or William or Henry? It nearly drives me mad to hear it, and all the other cats round here laugh at me because of it.

"It's getting dark now and she's out there rattling the biscuit packet - she'll be very lucky, I don't think. Good, she's given up and gone in; bet they're not speaking to one another. So far everything has gone to plan."

Next morning:

"They're still calling for me. I think they've asked good old Keith to feed me. The cat flap's left open and I can come and go as I please. The woman at the cattery won't like that - she will have lost a booking, busiest time too. Still, that's nothing to do with me!

"There they go, car loaded to bursting point, kids quarrelling, and the silly dog barking its head off.

"Right, I'll slip through the flap into the kitchen and have a good feed. Oh, there's nothing there. Come on Keith, get your act together or those koi carp will mysteriously disappear. What's that noise on the drive?

"Oh no, they are back already! He's tearing his hair out. It's the satellite navigation. It's taken them round the block and back here to the front door. He's blaming her and says she's meddled with it behind his back. She claims it was the dog nudged it with his nose. Why ever didn't they take me along to navigate? It's the dog who should have been left behind.

"I bet there's a smirk on Keith's face. I wondered what he was doing fiddling inside the car last night when they were calling for me. Bet he won't bother with satellite navigation now, waste of money.

"Off they go again. Come out from behind the bedroom curtains Keith, mission accomplished! That man's as two-faced as a kipper."

LAMENT AND CODA

DESPERATELY SEEKING DAISY *Norma Fulwood*

"Is that the RSPCA at Blackpool, please?"

"YES? Oh good! I want to give you one or two cat feeding bowls, water container, tray, cuddly bed and a few more things that a cat can consider belongs to him or her."

"Oh, I thought that somebody who perhaps can't afford such belongings for a cat would like them, and you'd know who that is."

"No! I've just lost Midge and I'm not going to have another cat."

"OK, I'll drop them in at the coffee morning and somebody will bring them to you from there."

****

"Oh, that'll be grand! I'll have the coffee ready tomorrow morning at about eleven, so that you won't be held up on your journey. Nice to have a chat, isn't it, for we haven't really done so for a long time, have we?"

****

"The poor little thing! Fancy having spent a month in Janet's back bedroom after having been thrown out like that. And knocked down and having a broken leg mended."

"You've got her in the car so you can't stay many minutes?"

"I quite agree. Mind you, you could bring her in and we can keep her with us in the kitchen. Then she can't get lost."

****

"What did you say her name was?"

"Daisy! Mmmmmmm ....

"She does seem to like this kitchen, doesn't she? Think I'll give her a drop of milk ....

.... Me, hooked again.

I toddled out to the shops and equipped Daisy with all the possessions that a lady cat should have. She was a truly loving cat. She liked sitting on a knee by the fire in winter and sitting in the sun in summer. One of her favourite spots was on the lawn underneath the almond tree. The early morning sun shone there, then moved around and there was no impediment to the sunshine for the whole of the day. When there was a chill in the air - but the sun shone - there was always a spot available between the plants on the table in the conservatory.

There were greenhouses in a field at the bottom of my garden and Daisy was very keen on sitting by a telegraph pole down there and watching the market gardener, Mr Wilcock (Norman), working either on or in the greenhouses. Mark you, she did her part in looking after the plants by catching a marauding mouse or two, except on Thursday mornings. That was when the fishmonger from Fleetwood delivered fish to the door at about 7.50 am. And Daisy certainly loved fresh fish!

On the occasion that a woman, daughter-in-law of a nearby nursery woman, told me that she, her dog and two cats had to sleep in a shed, as they had sold their house in Preston, it was winter. Her husband was scheduled to sleep on a settee at his mother's house, her daughter in the spare bedroom there, but she had been consigned to the shed. I told her that she and her animals could take over my study - with the patio door for an exit for the dog, if so required, during the night - so that is where she slept. After some time they bought a mobile home, in which they lived in a nearby field.

One day, when Daisy was sun-bathing, one of *her* cats, an un-neutered one, crept across the lawn and bit my Daisy in the back. Her life was despaired of by Tony her vet, but we brought her back to something like good condition after more than two years of careful nursing, medication and care. Bob cat was also bitten - in the eye - by the intruder, but his condition was much more speedily treated, and he was soon restored to good health. Daisy never was, really and truly, but she had had a far less healthy beginning. She remained her usual loving self.

One evening I heard a scuffle and saw Daisy shoot by the front door, pursued by the interloper. He was closely followed by Bob, who stopped him from attacking Daisy again. I understand that somehow or other the interloper returned home minus some fur on the undercarriage and various other places. He must surely have got involved in a fight.

Daisy took to sleeping in the guest room during the spring. The bed was comfortable and topped by a Welsh wool hand-made bedspread. Then she took to coming for supper, spending the night in her bedroom and leaving after breakfast every other day. Then she stopped coming.

With a few of my friends, and sometimes on my own, the fields, sheds and other buildings, etc, were scoured both visually and verbally, at all hours. I toured the immediate area and the nearby villages and properties, both looking and calling her name. The local vet, the local animal sanctuaries, and the homes of people I knew would offer a home to a lone dog or cat, were visited by me. The police, in addition to the above people, were given her chip particulars, to no avail.

One of the local sanctuaries gave me the phone number of a lady who, on her computer, circulates particulars of missing cats. She did a number of notices for me, which I distributed among the different shops in this and nearby villages, and posted in strategic spots on the road.

I would very much like Daisy to come home, as I still love her very much; failing that I hope she has found a very good home. Cats have been known to return home even after two years. One person told me that she knew of more than one cat that had been bitten on the back by an un-neutered cat and went missing. Does this have a long-term effect? If so, why?

LOST CATS - www.Mymoggy.com - FOUND CATS

(This is the website of Sue Nicholson, the lady whom Norma contacted when Daisy went missing.)

DAISY

Norma has also contributed to my first book - WAG TALES - published by d'Arblays Press. In that book she fondly recalls her much-loved dog, Peter, who grew up with her and her family during the years of the Second World War. She also tells about another dog she owned when she was older, Nipper, an abandoned Jack Russell.

BIMS INTELLIGENT CAT

P D Pemberton

This last little story, describing the friendship bond between pet cat and dog, has been submitted by P D Pemberton, a Devon writer who is also a supporter of ANIMALS ASIA and a tireless fund raiser for the charity.

P D Pemberton has also written a story, and three poems, in my recent book "WAG TALES - an Anthology of Rescued Dogs". Here is the story of Bims:

Bims was a sleek, slender tabby, a close friend of Roddie, our Scottie dog. She leaned against him to sleep at night.

When we had visitors, the two of them put on a demonstration for them. At the command "Off you go!" Bims raced round the garden, pursued by Roddie at full throttle a few feet behind. After 40 yards, at the end of the lawn, they both braked and stopped. Then they walked calmly away from each other. Visitors were impressed.

It was when she had kittens that her intelligence became apparent. The kittens had a nest in the bottom half of an open cupboard in the breakfast room, where she fed them.

One, still blind, came tottering out for adventure and staggered across the room to the steep step leading down to the kitchen. When it reached the step, mewing, Roddie recognized the hazard and rushed across to rescue it from the precipice. He carried it gently back in his mouth to its nest.

In succeeding days subsequent kittens started to explore. Roddie was kept busy all day retrieving and returning them to Bims. Relaxed, she lay back watching.

Her motto seemed to be: "Let your head save your feet."

FINALE

Chivers was not, strictly speaking, the first kitten to have lived in the office. There was another one, many years ago, that stayed for a brief time.

It was the evening of 1 October 1980. My mother, brother and myself were sitting quietly and sadly in the sitting room, talking over the events of the day. It was quiet after all the relatives, neighbours and friends had left. That morning we had laid Dad to rest in the churchyard behind our house. We were on our own. We knew we were to face a traumatic and difficult time in the days to come. We had been a very close family, just the four of us.

Dad had always loved animals, and cats were his special weakness. He had kept a black cat as a boy, but had developed asthma and the cat had had to go. We never had cats in the family, mum was not keen on them, but we had had dogs ever since I was eight years old.

Not long before he died Dad had said to me with great conviction, "You will always be all right if you have animals to look after!" In fact, over the years, he had made this remark on more than one occasion.

The door bell rang and I went to answer it. To my surprise there stood young Michael, the barmaid's son from the local pub, which Dad had frequented. Dad had always had a soft spot for this little boy and often used to buy him chocolate when he saw him waiting for his mother to leave work. Michael was holding a tiny black and white kitten. He held her up to me and said simply "Please take her in, Jenny, I couldn't think of anyone, only you. She's a stray and the older kids are throwing stones at her in the bus shelter."

I took her from him and he scampered off happily down the drive.

Later that night in bed, I thought of Dad, Michael, the kitten, and Dad's words. "You will always be all right if you have plenty of animals to look after." It all seemed linked, a reassuring message from Dad, that there would always be animals in need to care for. It was what I must keep on doing. Don't feel sad for too long, and all will be well.

But I did not keep Clementine, as I had named her. I kept her only for a few weeks, then Polly arrived on the scene and I felt that, with her and Asta, our wire fox terrier, we had enough pets. So Kate, our neighbour and a lover of cats, took her to Wales, to a friend who owned a farm and wanted a cat. Clementine lived there for many years and was happy.

Over the twenty-five years since Dad passed away we have owned twelve cats. Oliver was black and, I believe, belonged to a family who abandoned him when they left the area. I remember seeing the youngest boy kneeling beside Dad's grave, looking at all the flowers. Another link? Oliver came to us shortly afterwards.

Mimi, another black cat through Mary, a trusted friend, and again connected with family.

Even Phillip, who rang me up so concerned about Aubrey, was a friend from far-gone childhood days. Aubrey was our third black cat.

Cats have always had mystical associations and black cats are supposed to bring good luck. I know Mary, whose husband Robert was of Celtic origin, was very influenced by symbols, and good and bad luck signs.

Whether or not this is true, I wouldn't like to say. I do know that over the years all my pets have always been there for me, giving unconditional love and devotion and accepting me for myself.

Also, they provide endless amusement and entertainment. I only have to see young Chivers giving me one of his "hard stares" when things are not to his liking and this never fails to dispel a gloomy moment.

Non-judgmental and loyal, all of the many dogs and cats I have owned have been good companions through difficult times, providing the unique, silent support that only dumb creatures are able to offer when we need comforting most.

Jenny Fensom
Good Companions
Streatley, Bedfordshire

2006

AFTERWORD

David Neale - *Animals Asia Foundation*

Animals have always been my number one passion and Cats share a very special place in my heart, alongside the many other animals that I have shared my life with. Working for the protection of animals means that there are many highs and lows throughout life. The highs come from meeting animals which have been saved from a life of misery and are now free to roam inside a happy and stable home environment. The lows come from seeing the look on the faces of animals, so desperately in need of our help, when we can not act immediately to change their destiny.

Cats certainly deserve a place in all of our hearts and, just like other animals, they deserve to be loved and protected from harm. At Animals Asia Foundation we are working with Asian people who really do care about cats, dogs and all animals just as much as we cat and dog lovers care about our companion animals. It is these people, and their hope and commitment to create change, that will change the destiny of the many millions of companion animals which are so cruelly killed for their food and fur. This provides us all with the hope that one day we will see an end to the despicable markets which hold cats and dogs in filthy, disgusting conditions, ready to be killed for their food and fur.

By purchasing this book you have helped in some small way to continue the essential animal welfare work that Animals Asia Foundation is carrying out across Asia, helping to change people's opinions about all animals, as we move towards a more compassionate society, and one which sees cats as our friends and companions, to be loved and cared for.

Thank you.

David Neale
UK Director
Animals Asia Foundation

dneale@animalsasia.org